RELIGIONS OF THE WORLD

Published in 1996 by
Marshall Cavendish Corporation
99 White Plains Road
Tarrytown, NY 10591-9001
U.S.A.

Editor: Henk Dijkstra
Executive Editor: Paulien Retèl
Revision Editors: Rob van den Berg (Hinduism), Frits Naerebout (The Buddha, Buddhism, Early Chinese Thinkers),
Henk Singor (The Jewish People, Christianity, Christianity Comes of Age, The Fall of Paganism, Christian Theology and Popular
Belief, Monasticism, The Church in the West)
Art Director: Henk Oostenrijk, Studio 87, Utrecht, The Netherlands
Index Editors: Schuurmans & Jonkers, Leiden, The Netherlands
Preface: Suzanne Heim, Ph.D., Ancient Near East and Classical Art and Archaeology

The History of the Ancient and Medieval World is a completely revised and
updated edition of *The Adventure of Mankind*.
©1996 HD Communication Consultants BV, Hilversum, The Netherlands
This edition © 1996 by Marshall Cavendish Corporation, Tarrytown,
New York and HD Communication Consultants BV, Hilversum, The Netherlands

Library of Congress Cataloging-in-Publication Data

History of the ancient and medieval world / edited by Henk Dijkstra.
p. cm.
Completely rev. and updated ed. of :The Adventure of mankind (second edition 1996).
Contents:—v.7. Religions of the World.
ISBN 0-7614-0358-2 (v.7).—ISBN 0-7614-0351-5 (lib.bdg.:set)
1. History, Ancient—Juvenile literature. 2. Middle Ages—History—Juvenile literature. I. Dijkstra, Henk. II. Title: Adventure of mankind.
D117.H57 1996
930—dc20/95-35715

History of the
Ancient & Medieval World

Volume 7

Religions
of the World

Marshall Cavendish
New York   Toronto   Sydney

Religions of the World

Hinduist painting from the seventeenth century depicting the Hindu god Krishna on the left.

CONTENTS

Preface

From the sixth century BC to the fourth century AD, several new currents of religious thought developed. In contrast to the polytheism of ancient cults, in which adherents worshiped a number of gods, many of the new religions were either monotheistic—as in Judaism and Christianity—or based on the concept of an impersonal god—as in Buddhism and Daoism (Taoism).

In India the Brahmanistic beliefs that would develop into Hinduism have been traced to the Indo-European settlers in the northeast of the subcontinent. The historical figure of Buddha, Siddhartha Gautama, is believed to have lived during the sixth century BC, teaching that life is suffering and liberation is achieved through self-purification. Buddhism was adopted as the official religion of the empire of Asoka in the third century BC and spread east to China, Southeast Asia, Korea, and Japan, where it developed into several different variants, or "vehicles." The most important of these are Mahayana, or "great vehicle," and Ch'an, or Zen.

Buddhism in East Asia competed with Confucianism and Daoism. The Confucianism of the Chinese philosopher Confucius was a humanistic moral philosophy in favor around 500 BC. Daoism, based on the teachings of the legendary Lao-tzu, is also thought to have originated about 500 BC. Where Confucianism focused on proper actions, Daoism held metaphysical ideas about the natural flow of events. As Buddhism penetrated the upper echelons of Chinese society in the early centuries AD, it turned away from asceticism, adopting some of the moral aspects of Confucianism, the metaphysics of Daoism, and Chinese ideas about the cosmos.

In 598 BC the Babylonian king Nebuchadnezzar II took over Jerusalem and deported its Jewish elite to his kingdom. In the late sixth and early fifth centuries BC, many Jews returned to Jerusalem and rebuilt the temple. However, after the conquest of Judaea by Alexander the Great in the fourth century BC, many of the prominent Jews adopted Greek customs and abandoned traditional ways, separating into factions that disagreed about the acceptance of Greek culture and religion. After the Maccabee revolt of 164 BC Jerusalem was ruled by a Jewish council of priests and religious leaders, but there was disagreement over acceptance of foreign conquerors and doctrines. In the first century Jewish Zealots revolted against the Roman Empire, while the Essenes withdrew completely.

Christianity grew out of the divisions within Judaism. In the centuries following the death of Jesus of Nazareth, Christianity spread throughout the Roman Empire. Roman emperors attempted to suppress Christianity, which was eventually adopted as the official religion of the empire and later the leading religion of Europe. Although the Jews of Judaea would be dispersed throughout the world, their precepts ensured a cohesive religion. Islam would replace Christianity in much of North Africa and western Asia in the seventh century AD, and while the practice of Buddhism in India waned in favor of Hinduism, it remained a major influence throughout the rest of Asia.

Suzanne Heim, Ph.D.
Ancient Near East and Classical Art and Archaeology

The Buddha

Entering Nirvana

Although the date is not certain, it is generally believed that Siddhartha Gautama, the man known as the Buddha (the "Enlightened One"), was born about 563 BC in Lumbini Grove next to Kapilavastu. His father was head of the Sakya clan, members of the Kshatriya caste. This led to the Buddha being called Sakyamuni (Sage of the Sakyas). In the Brahmanic religion of the family, the caste comprised warriors and rulers. Above it were the Brahmans, the priests. Below it were those of the Vaishya caste, who made up most of the general public, and their servants of the Shudra caste. These social layers and the Brahmanism that defined them had been brought to the subcontinent by Indo-Europeans about 1500 BC. (The Shudra caste was defined after they had settled in the valley of the Ganges River.

Below the rungs of the caste ladder were the Untouchables, considered outside the system.) The religion would develop into Hinduism, named for the Sanskrit word *sindhu* (river), specifically the Indus River.

By the time Siddhartha was born, most of the Brahmanic texts called the *Vedas* had been written, drawing the hymns and rituals of the religion from centuries of oral tradition. (The *Upanishads*, philosophical meditations concerning the meaning of existence, were written after the sixth century BC.)

Painting on cloth representing Buddha with his disciples. The painting is kept in a museum in Sri Lanka.

871

Gilded wooden
statue of Buddha, probably
made in Korea

Picture representing
the birth of Buddha. According
to legend, Queen Maya dreamed of a god
in the form of a white elephant.
Ten months later her son Gautama was
born, later to be known as Buddha.

Central to Brahmanism was belief in transmigration, the notion that the human soul is reborn in an endless cycle of death and rebirth. Legend says that at his birth, Gautama said, "This is my last existence."

It was a time of socioeconomic and cultural transition in India. The use of iron was spreading, cities were developing, and farmers were trying new methods of irrigation. Commerce changed as merchants adopted silver and copper coinage on the Persian model. A certain religious disquiet existed, as well. New religious movements began to compete with Brahmanism, objecting to its ritualistic nature, its sacrifices, and its elitism. All these concerns would be shared by Gautama.

Siddhartha Gautama was married at the age of sixteen to a cousin from a neighboring country. The wedding was arranged (this was a common practice then and now in India) for political reasons. His wife gave birth to a son, assuring the continuation of the dynasty.

When the prince was twenty-nine years old, according to legend, he was riding with his shield bearer named Chanda when he saw an old man and asked, "Who is that man with white hair, dull eyes, and trembling body?"

"It is an old man," replied Chanda. "He was once a child who lay at his mother's breast, and later a young man full of life. But now his bloom has faded, and he has lost his strength."

"And how can a person experience enjoyment when he knows that he will soon be old and useless?" Gautama wondered. Then he saw another man sitting beside the road and asked, "What is wrong with him?"

"He is ill," said Chanda. "The organs of his body have failed. We are all subject to daily malfunctions." Using his whip, he hurried the horses along to spare his master the unpleasant sight, but they soon encountered a funeral procession.

"What are those people carrying among the flowers?" the prince asked.

Chanda replied, "They are accompanying a corpse. His limbs are stiff, his thoughts have left him, he no longer lives. His joys and his sorrows are over. Everything must die; it is not possible to escape death."

These encounters with old age, illness, and death are said to have formed Gautama's

Picture of a Buddhist relief dating from the second century BC. It represents the Siddhartha Gautama about to take leave of his life in the palace.

view of suffering as the common experience of humankind. When he subsequently met an itinerant ascetic, serene in his rejection of earthly attachments, Gautama decided to try that way of life. The event is still celebrated by Buddhists as the Great Renunciation. Leaving his family and privileged life, he set out on a search for truth as a mendicant.

He studied with two yoga masters and devoted himself to meditation and other ascetic practices. After six years of extreme self-denial he also rejected asceticism, finding that it had not led to his enlightenment. Although he had attracted five disciples who now abandoned him, he chose a middle path, a lifestyle neither indulgent nor self-denying.

About 528, meditating under a *bo* (pipal) tree in the forest of Bodh Gaya (in the modern Indian state of Bihar), he reached the goal he sought. He meditated all night, ridding himself of his "outflows" (ignorance and desire), the influences of the god Mara. Moving through rising levels of conscious-

Statuette of a gazelle kneeling in admiration for the preaching Buddha. The horn is a symbol of nirvana.

873

ness, he finally understood the Four Noble Truths, attaining the Great Enlightenment. Surrounded by miraculous signs, he announced that he was the Buddha.

Convinced by the god Brahma, it is said, the doubtful Buddha decided to make his teachings known out of compassion for humankind. He traveled to Benares (Varanasi), where he gave his first sermon in the Deer Park to the five fellow seekers of truth he had known in his days as an ascetic. Its text has been preserved. Presenting the essence of Buddhism, it did as it was defined, "Setting in motion the wheel of the Doctrine."

The Four Noble Truths

In describing the way of salvation from suffering, the Buddha said first, "This is the Noble Truth concerning sorrow. Birth is sorrow, age is sorrow . . . death is sorrow." His point here was more than that suffering is a part of life; it is existence itself, unrelieved even by death because death is followed by further rebirth.

In the Second Truth, he said that all suffering comes from ignorance. Desire, or the craving of and attachment to the pleasures of life, is caused by that ignorance.

In the Third, he claimed that suffering can be ended by ending ignorance and desire.

In the Fourth Truth, he detailed the way to

A Nepalese miniature dating from the tenth century AD. It represents the moment in which Gautama achieves Enlightenment.

Gautama was married to his cousin Yasodhara. This mural from Sri Lanka depicts the wedding ceremony.

874

end suffering, described as eight steps on a path: right views, right resolve, right speech, right action, right livelihood, right effort, right mindfulness, and right concentration.

"Verily, I say to you, this is the Noble Eightfold Path: the right vision, free of superstition and illusions; the right desires, high-minded and worthy of an intelligent person; the right honest and true word; the right behavior, in peace, honesty, and purity; the right actions, without being harmful to life; the right efforts, which lead to control; the right spirit, active, observant, and awake; the right contemplation, which makes us meditate the reality of life.

"And with regard to suffering, there are five things which cause pain. These are: birth, illness, death, contact with pleasant things, and the withdrawal of pleasant things. Those five are the result of the composition of our body. This is the cause of pain. We seek the rejuvenation of that which is constantly changing, either by a life after death or a greater intensity of our life on earth. This, then, is the truth with regard to the annihilation of pain; the Noble Eightfold Path: the right vision, the right desires, the right word, the right behavior, the right actions, the right efforts, the right spirit, and the right meditation.

"For a long time I was unable to clearly differentiate these values; for a long time I understood that I had not obtained total wisdom. But now I have achieved the highest knowledge, and a light has gone on inside of me. My will has been liberated, this is my last existence.

"He who lives alone, though he may have recognized the truth, can waver and return to his old habits. Therefore it would behoove us to join together to help and support one another. Be as brothers, join together in love, in holiness, and in striving. Preach the doctrine through the four spheres of the world, so that all creatures become brothers in the realm of truth. This is the holy fraternity where they shall live in unity, those who have found a solace in the Buddha."

These eight steps can be categorized as morality, wisdom, and mindful concentration. Called *samadhi*, this concentration is achieved through meditation. Through the insight gained through meditation, Buddha said, one can learn to avoid two extremes. One of these is that of sensual pleasure and the other is that of self–castigation through painful habits which only confound us and which are not advantageous to us. There is a middle path, a path which will open our eyes to understanding and bring us peace, because it brings us to wisdom, to truth, to nirvana. Buddha had simply found that path

and shown it to others. He is like the physician who knows the cause and the treatment of the disease—the disease of existence. The physician makes recommendations; but the healing of the patient depends upon himself.

The *Tathagata*

The Buddha spent the next forty-five years after his appearance in Benares as an itinerant teacher, collecting followers, and establishing *sanghas* (monasteries). His first disciples were the five ascetics who had

rejoined him in Benares. They were the first Buddhist monks. Once his ranks rose to sixty, he sent the monks out to spread the Doctrine along the Ganges Valley, between the cities of Allahabad and Patna in northeastern India. In these intentional communities he created, the Buddha admitted women as well as men from all castes. Their intent was right action. The Buddha had some help from his father here. Returning home for a while, he converted his father, his wife, and other relatives. The first monasteries were formed under royal protection. After the death of his father, his widow, the stepmother of Buddha, and her companions joined a monastery, becoming the first nuns.

This strong missionary drive remained

Stone relief representing a Bodhisattva (a future Buddha) on a throne

part of Buddhist tradition. He told his followers to "go forth . . . for the help of the many, for the well-being of the many, out of compassion for the world." The third-century BC Indian king Asoka converted and sent his own missionaries out. They reached several places in Southeast Asia. The religion the Buddha founded would eventually reach Tibet and Nepal, Mongolia, China, Japan, and Korea. However, in India, its

he is a universal ruler who reigns over the universe with the wheel of the Doctrine, first set in motion in Benares. In this view he surpasses the gods themselves, rising above causation. They see this omniscient Buddha as the "Teacher of gods and man."

The Buddha taught a concept of *nirvana* that encompasses the notions of both fulfillment and emptiness. Taken from a word that means "blown out," nirvana is the extinction of the cycle of rebirths, reached when the individual overcomes every form of attachment to worldly aspirations and desires. When he was about eighty, the Buddha traveled to Kushinagara in Nepal. In 483 BC, after a brief illness (reportedly from eating tainted pork), he reached that state of "total blowing-out" and entered nirvana. Amid extensive ceremonies, his body was cremated by the local prince. Buddhist tradition maintains that his ashes were divided into 84,000 units and distributed among the main followers who installed them in *stupas* (relic shrines). The Buddha had become the Tathagata (he who reached the state of perfection).

Represented in this mural in an Ajanta grotto in Decan is a female dancer. There are twenty-nine artificial grottos in Ajanta. They were carved during the period from 100 BC to the fifth century AD.

homeland, Buddhism disappeared around the twelfth century.

The three main aspects of Buddhism, the Buddha himself, his teachings, and the monastic orders, are called its "Three Jewels." An important question is what kind of being the Buddha was in the eyes of his followers. Schools arose within Buddhism, over the course of time, that placed great emphasis on what they saw as his superhuman characteristics. Some of these virtually strip the Buddha of all humanity, presenting him as more on the order of a cosmic principle, the embodiment of transcendental wisdom and truth. Others claim the Buddha was more than simply a human teacher. To them,

Greenish limestone carving of a Buddhist stupa, a dome-shaped stone shrine built to house relics, from Nagarjunakonda, India (third century AD)

Buddhism

Dharma: *The Buddhist Teachings*

Siddhartha Gautama, the man called the Buddha, made no claim to divinity. He was exclusively an oral teacher and his disciples passed on his concepts in the same way, aided by the lives they shared in monasteries. Not until the first century BC were his teachings written down. Together they are called the *Dharma*, the way to enlightenment.

Basic to the *Dharma* are the Four Noble Truths. Described in some detail in the last chapter, these postulate that existence is suffering; that suffering is caused by ignorance of the true nature of reality, leading to attach-

877

ment and craving for worldly pleasures; that suffering can be overcome; and that the way to end suffering can be learned by following the Eightfold Path to spiritual improvement. This, in brief, consists of right views, right intention, right speech, right action, right livelihood, right effort, right mindfulness, and right concentration.

The Buddha rejected the manifold gods of Hinduism, although he did not specifically deny their existence. He considered them subject to death and rebirth as lower crea-

tures rather than beings in charge of human fate. He did not consider prayer or sacrifice to them to be of any value. Rather than presenting an alternative concept of a divinity himself, Buddha saw Enlightenment, inner understanding, as a matter of individual human effort. Insight could be achieved through meditation, and was therefore potentially possible for everyone. "Seek in the

impersonal for the eternal man," he said, "and having sought him out, look inward— thou art Buddha."

Buddha's Doctrines
Anatman

Buddha denied the existence of an enduring self or soul like that called *atman* in Hinduism. Hence his doctrine postulates *anatman* (no soul). According to this doctrine, people were made up of impermanent combinations of elements or bundles, called *skandhas*. These included the body, emotions, perceptions, volition, and consciousness. The concept of an immortal personality is recorded as an illusion that led to self-centeredness, craving, and suffering. *Anitya* (impermanence) is seen as being as basic to existence as *duhkha* (suffering).

He taught that a chain of causation was what determined individual makeup. Called *pratityasamutpada* (dependent origin), the doctrine holds that each link in the chain is determined by the previous one and becomes a prerequisite for the next. The first link is ignorance, the cause of suffering. Ignorance

The Bodhnath stupa, in the valley of Kathmandu. Typical for Nepal are the eyes that can be seen on the stupa; perhaps they are a symbol of the all-seeing Buddha, but the interpretations still vary.

Upper part of one of the many columns that Asoka had placed in his empire, this one shaped as a lion. Today this is still a symbol of India.

878

leads to the "will to live," a prerequisite for the consciousness of the mind and the senses. The mind determines the "name and form," the visible and invisible qualities of the human being. The senses enable contact with the outside world, which leads to perception, then desire, and finally, attachment to existence. Existence brings birth, old age, death, and rebirth. There is a connection from life to life, but not in the Hindu sense of transmigration, since the atman is only a series of five transitory aggregates moving through the cycle of phenomenal existence termed *samsara*.

Karma

Pratityasamutpada is related to Buddha's concept of *karma* (act or deed), one's acts and their consequences in a subsequent existence. Karma is akin to fate; one's karma decides his personal attributes, appearance, intelligence, caste, even his species. Buddha said there were "five destinations" or possibilities: rebirth in hell, as a "starving spirit," as an animal, as a human, or as a god. Karma is inevitable and unavoidable, not a matter of divine judgment but of cause and effect.

The present life is determined by the past. However, in Buddhism one's actions in the present life are not fated. One can choose those actions, modifying behavior to affect karma. Adopting the four right attitudes is essential. These are compassion, kindness, sympathetic joy, and equanimity. Buddha offered five moral precepts that prohibited killing, theft, hurtful language, sexual misconduct, and the use of intoxicants.

Nirvana

The goal is release from karma, liberation from the cycle of samsara, or endless rebirth. It is called *Nirvana* (blow out). To Buddha it meant blowing out the fires of desire, hatred, and ignorance, reaching a condition of complete detachment. It did not mean annihilation, but rather the attainment of the epitome of consciousness.

It was said that the Buddha refused to answer questions about the nature of the universe or Nirvana, considering it pointless to think about these things. He spoke instead about how Nirvana could be reached. "Do not concern yourself with what one must know or what one must say," he explained. "How can you benefit from the . . . habit of a monk if bad thoughts make you impure?" He also considered it vain to seek the beginning and end of things. "A religious life does not depend on the question of whether the world is infinite or finite, nor whether or not we exist after death. . . . When the fire goes out, do you perhaps ask yourself if it has gone to the north or to the south, or to the east or to the west?"

Sangha

Although theoretically anyone could attain Nirvana by following the Eightfold Path, Buddha believed that people freed of worldly cares had a better chance of succeeding. He felt that life in a *sangha* (monastic order) provided a realistic way to achieve the goal, not that a monk was a better person. The monk was not intended to effect the liberation of others but to strive for his own liberation. Monasteries were open, in principle, to men and women alike, from any walk of life and any caste, but escaped slaves, debtors, soldiers, and people in the service of a sovereign were excluded.

The monk is subject to strict discipline, which can vary considerably from one school of thought to another. However, no monk is permitted to have sexual relations, to steal, to kill, or to feign supernatural power. Infractions of these four rules are punished by expulsion. There are also innumerable regulations for daily life. Joining a novitiate is simple: Shaving the hair on the head, putting on a habit, and making a decla-

The great stupa of Sanchi, India. Its present form dates from the first century BC. One of the four entrance gates can be seen in front of the stupa. However, the stupa is not supposed to be entered; it is a massive construction, based on the shape of Indian burial mounds, and a symbol of Buddha's *parinirvana*, leaving the world behind.

879

The great temple of
Angkor Wat in Cambodia

ration in the presence of an older monk are
sufficient. The ordination is a ceremonial
occasion, involving extensive questioning
and the assumption of a new name to symbolize a break with one's old life. Monastic
life is ascetic, but not extreme. Monks are
allowed only the simplest possessions and
are expected to beg for other things. Once
the daily begging is over, monks return to
the community, spending the rest of the day
and much of the night in spiritual exercise.
Any form of work is forbidden.

The *sangha* was dependent on the laity,
since the monks themselves were, in principle, unproductive. This tradition has had
many repercussions. Because the greatest
"giver" was often the sovereign, Buddhism
entered the political world, occasionally
becoming a state religion. Although monks
were allowed to own virtually nothing, the
monastic community as a collective could
accept generous donations, particularly land.
A monastery could own land worked by lay
farmers who gave part of the harvest to the

monks. At certain times and places monks
also engaged in commercial activities.
Monasteries were also situated around the
main relic shrines, which soon became pil-
grimage centers.

The Buddhist Canon

The literature of Buddhism, transmitted orally until the first century BC, was written in
Sanskrit but no complete text exists except in
the dialect Pali. Consisting of three collections of writings, the canon is called *Tripitaka* (Three Baskets). The *Sutra Pitaka*,
conversations between people and the
Buddha, is itself made up of five *Nikaya*
(collections): *Digha* (Long Discourses),
Majjhima (Medium-length Discourses), *Sa-
myutta* (Grouped Discourses), *Anguttara*
(Discourses on Numbered Topics), and
Khuddaka (Miscellaneous Texts). The *Vinaya Pitaka* contains some 225 monastic
regulations, citing the reason for each. The
Abhidharma Pitaka contains seven texts
treating psychological, metaphysical, and
technical matters.

Schisms

After the death of the Buddha, his followers
met in council at Rajagriha (today Rajgir) to
recite and review what he had taught them,
seeking agreement on and recording his
words, including those on monastery rules
(*vinaya*). About 383 BC, those rules formed

‹ Gray schist head
of Buddha, found at Gandhara,
from the third or fourth
century BC

881

An entrance
to the temple of
Angkor Wat

the agenda for a second council at Vaishali. The monks of the Vajjian Confederacy had taken to using money, drinking wine, and violating other norms. The council banned the practices, but not unanimously. Either then or some thirty years later, a schism occurred between the liberal *Mahasanghikas* (Great Assembly) and the more conservative *Sthaviras* (Elders).

The Mahasanghikas had come to a different understanding of the nature of Buddha. Rather than regarding him as simply a human teacher who had found enlightenment, they contended that the Buddha was eternal, that the human, Siddhartha Gautama, had been created as an apparition of the transcendent Buddha to help people understand him. This concept reappears in the later form of Buddhism, Mahayana. Eventually, what are called the Eighteen Schools of Old Buddhism developed. Only one of those, Theravada, still exists.

Theravada

Theravada (the Way of the Elders) is also called *Shravakayana* (the Vehicle of the Disciples) or *Hinayana* (the Lesser Vehicle), a derogatory term that its followers do not accept.

To the Theravadin, the sangha is all-important in following the Eightfold Path. Laypeople, unlikely to achieve Nirvana, gain merit by their support of the monks. Monks who attain Enlightenment (reaching Nirvana does not require death) are called *arhats* (saints). Although the Buddha is not actually

Details from the temple of
Banteay Srei (from the end of the
tenth century) in Angkor,
Cambodia

Stele depicting the Buddha performing the great miracle at Shravasti. This Gandharan relief from the second or third century AD exhibits the influence of Greco-Roman art.

Entrance to
Cave I at Ajanta

The so-called
face towers of the Bayon
temple in Angkor

worshiped, he is venerated or honored in the Theravada stupa cult. A stupa is a dome-shaped stone shrine built to house Buddhist relics, like the tooth of Buddha in Kandy, Sri Lanka.

Theravadins regard the *Tripitaka* as the record of the remembered sayings of the historical Buddha, Gautama. They also had commentaries on the Canon and Compendia of doctrine. One is the *Visudhim (Path of Purification)*, a manual for meditators.

Mahayana

Between the second century BC and the first century AD, another school of Buddhism developed, called *Mahayana* (the Greater Vehicle). It postulates a Buddha characterized by *trikaya* (the three-bodied aspect). The "body of essence," formless, unchanging, and absolute, is the ultimate consciousness, the essential Buddha. The "body of communal bliss" has a godlike form in the heavens. In the "body of transformation," the Buddha appears in human form on earth to show humans his truth. Siddhartha Gautama was only one of countless examples. Mahayana offers salvation equally to monk and layperson. Its goal is not only Nirvana but self-sacrifice and compassion. The ideal being is not the arhat of Theravada but the *bodhisattva* (enlightened being) who, on the threshold of Nirvana, postpones entry to help others to the same insight he or she has. He or she can transfer the merit earned over many lives to others less fortunate. This led to a deification of some bodhisattvas, considered possible future manifestations of Buddha.

Prayer, often chanted, and ritual are very important in Mahayana Buddhism. Statues and portraits of Buddha and bodhisattvas are objects of devotion in temples and private homes. Scripture is less traditional, not tied to the Tripitaka.

Later Developments from Mahayana

Mahayanins did not regard the extant canon of Buddhism, the *Tripitaka*, as carrying the same authority accorded it by the Theravadins. In the Theravada view, these texts were attributed to the Buddha himself. Mahayanists considered them "temporary" teachings, not invalid but not final. Finding the old dogma lacking, they sought new texts. These include the *Avatamsaka Sutra*

(Garland Sutra), the *Lankavatara Sutra*, and the writings called the *Prarjnaparamita (Perfection of Wisdom)*. They also developed new sects over the centuries.

The *Saddharmapundarika Sutra (Lotus of the True Doctrine Sutra or Lotus Sutra)* is considered by the Japanese sect called *Nichiren* to define the essence of Buddhism. The sect, named for its thirteenth-century founder, has gained significant popularity in Japan over the last forty years. Its lay association, *Soka Gakkai* (Value Creation Society), uses mass media to win converts. Its political party, *Komeito* (Clean Government) has run candidates for office.

About 520, the Indian Bodhidharma introduced Ch'an Buddhism to China. The same word in Sanskrit is *dhyana*. This is the state of consciousness of a Buddha, a person who has achieved the state where the mind no longer clings to (or desires) the material world of experience. The Chinese called this experience *wu-xin* (no mind). Its basis was the Buddhist "Doctrine of Pure Being." Here the central thought is that all phenomena are the product of the consciousness. The way to liberation comes down to a purification of that consciousness. Sensory perception no longer interferes with absolute truth.

Siddhartha Gautama spoke about this state as achievable by practiced meditation and personal effort. Tantrists taught that repetition of phrases (mantras) could lend focus to one's meditation. Zen discards such attempts at spiritual exercise and claims that salvation (a liberated mind) can only come from sud-

Statue of glazed stone from China (Liao dynasty, AD 907–1125).
A *lohan*, the Chinese name for an arhat, a Buddhist monk who has reached Enlightenment

den insight. This is called *satori* in Japanese. Recognition that even one's own self is not distinct, but relative, is essential. By realizing the underlying unity of reality through a sort of internal about-face, Zen says it is possible to become immune to the impulses of the senses and to experience pure consciousness, the world "just as it is." This is said to be identical to the nature of Buddhahood.

By the technique called direct pointing, answering philosophical questions with simple words or actions, the Zen master attempts to share the vision he or she has with stu-

The Spread of Buddhism in the Far East

dents, who try to understand through *zazen* (meditation) the quiet observation of "what is." There are two major Zen sects in Japan today, both introduced by Japanese monks studying in China. Eisai created the Rinzai sect in 1191, and Dogen introduced the Soto sect in 1227. They have had great influence on the art, poetry, and culture of the country.

Amidism, or Pure Land Doctrine, like Ch'an, originated in China and was carried to Japan and east Asia. It emphasizes belief in a transcendent, compassionate Buddha called Amida (*Amitabha* in Sanskrit). Through endless repetition of "Homage to the Buddha Amida" (although in theory, once will do), they prove devotion, trying to

gain rebirth in the paradise "Pure Land."

Vajrayana

In the seventh century AD, another school of Buddhism developed in north India out of Mahayana and folkloric beliefs. Called *Vajrayana* (the Diamond Vehicle), or Buddhist Tantrism, it has a strong mystical orientation, based mainly on *tantras*, texts about mysticism, magic, and *mudras* (secret rituals). (The Tantric movement arose about the same time in Hinduism.) It is characterized by a very personal bond between student and teacher, *mandalas* (maps) or circles symbolizing the universe, and *mantras* (sacred syllables) chanted to focus meditation. Introduced in Tibet by the Indian monk Padmasambhava in AD 747, it became the predominant religion there. At about the fifteenth century its members began to regard the lamas or abbots of its monasteries as reincarnations of bodhisattvas, designating the foremost one of them, the Dalai Lama, a ruler of the country. This theocracy was ended only when China seized Tibet in 1950. The present Dalai Lama lives in exile in India.

Asoka (c.291–232 BC), King (c.273–232 BC) of Magadha

The formation of new schools of thought was no hindrance to the further spread of Buddhism. Its greatest impetus came from the actions of King Asoka in the third century BC. The third king of the Mauryan dynasty, he was a grandson of its founder Chandragupta, who had subdued northwest India, driving out the Greek garrisons left after Alexander's retreat. Asoka expanded his kingdom, conquering most of the Indian subcontinent. He was stopped only in the far south. About 270 BC he became acquainted with Buddhism. By 261 BC he had seized the state of Kalinga in a particularly brutal conquest. Overcome by remorse for the suffering he had caused, he renounced warfare and Brahmanism in favor of Buddhism. Although its doctrine of *ahimsa* (nonviolence) especially attracted him, Asoka also instituted Buddhist principles of compassion in social reforms for the peasants. He had medical centers built, wells dug, and trees planted. He set up medical services for animals, forbade cruel treatment of them, and regulated (but did not forbid) their slaughter. Asoka did not persecute or even forbid other religions, but he did have great interest in missionary work. He built monasteries and shrines and had sayings of the Buddha engraved on rocks and monuments.

An existing stone engraving made at his decree states: "After eight years of rule, the

887

king decided to conquer Kalinga, and 150,000 people were sold as slaves. Another 100,000 were killed in the battles, and even more died as a result of the war. But immediately after the annexation of Kalinga, the king felt the need to protect the doctrine and to expand the knowledge of it to those who did not know it. The conquest of Kalinga caused intense pain and remorse in the king. This, then, was the greatest conquest of the king: the conquest of the Doctrine of

Reliefs at the entrance of Cave IX in Ajanta

Compassion; and so he worked to spread the doctrine to 600 miles (965 kilometers) past the borders, by sending out missions from his country to King Antiochus, and to the four kings who lived north of Antiochus, to the kings of the south. . . . This is the only conquest which fills one with happiness: the conquest of the doctrine. The king viewed only that which bears fruit for the other life as something which bears fruit. For this reason he wrote this edict, and also so that his sons and his grandsons would not feel obligated to take over new areas. And if for any reason they were forced to take up their weapons, they were to do so with patience and goodness and always remember that real conquests are made by compassion; this applies to our present life and to our future one."

< One of four entrance gates of the Great Stupa of Sanchi, India

The Spread of Buddhism

At about 250 BC Asoka's son Mahendra, a monk, took Theravada Buddhism to Sri Lanka, where it remains the dominant religion. According to tradition, it was carried from Sri Lanka to Myanmar (formerly Burma) during Asoka's reign, but the first evidence of it only appears there in the fifth century AD. Within a century it had spread to Thailand, where it was eventually adopted as the official religion. It is still strong in both Myanmar and Thailand today. In Cambodia and Laos, where Buddhism was made the state religion in the fourteenth century, it is popular with the people but has been rejected by the governments.

Buddhism declined in the land of its origin, India, but prospered in various forms elsewhere in Asia. In the fourth century AD, most of India experienced a period of cultural flourishing in which both Buddhism and Brahmanism played a part. In the sixth and seventh centuries, Buddhism came under pressure, particularly in the west and parts of southern India, from a revival of Brahmanism that led to the development of classical Hinduism. The final blow, however, came from Islam. Islamic Turks conquered all of northern India in the twelfth century, pushing Buddhism out to a few peripheral areas. It has recently made a comeback. Since 1956, the Indian Bhimrao Ramji Ambedkar has converted some 3.5 million members of the so-called Untouchable caste to Buddhism.

In the first century AD, Mahayana Buddhism reached China via the traders' Silk Route. Opposed by Confucianists, it still became part of Chinese culture, mutually influencing and being influenced by it. A new Buddhist sect, Ch'an (or Zen in Japan), was introduced about 520 by the Indian monk Bodhidharma. After the last great persecution in 845 (there were others in 446 and 574–577), Buddhism outside that sect faded in China. All religion in China today is subject to strict control by the Communist government.

Mahayana Buddhism reached Vietnam in the second century, Korea in the fourth, and Japan (officially, although earlier contact is probable) in 552. Prince Shotoku made it the religion of his kingdom in 593. Zen Buddhism, from the Chinese sect Ch'an, became very popular in the twelfth century and has many followers today.

Hinduism

The Religion
of India

The history of Hinduism goes back four millennia to the arrival of the first believers in Brahman, the source of universal life. They were Indo-Aryan people, moving into the foothills of the Himalayas from somewhere near the Caspian Sea. Part of the Indo-European migrations to India begun 6,000 years earlier, they carried with them the concepts and traditions that would help form the religion named for the Indus River (*Sindhu* in Sanskrit). With no generally accepted dogma (or system of religious teaching), no creed, and no centralized hierarchy of priests, Hinduism has some 700 million adherents today. They define themselves as those who believe in the *Vedas*, the oldest Indian writings. From its inception, the religion was a fusion of a great variety of concepts and observances, local deities and rites of worship from an enormous number of cultures.

Historical Background

Between 1800 and 1200 BC, the nomadic Indo-Aryans established themselves in the Indus Valley. The Indo-Aryans' earliest cross-cultural contact may have been with

the native inhabitants. The culture of the indigenous inhabitants, although in decline, was a more settled and urbanized way of life than their own, but the Indo-Aryans had greater military power and faster spike-wheeled horse drawn chariots, were well-organized for conquest, as well as being skilled in agriculture and animal husbandry. It is probable that the Indus Valley culture had already been weakened by natural calamities or epidemics over the period of 2000–1750 BC.

The native people met by the Indo-Aryans were anything but primitive, according to early twentieth-century excavations. They built cities according to architectural plans, something done only in some cities in Babylonia at that time. Two cities that have been excavated, Harappa and Mohenjo-Daro

Indian painting from c. 1730 depicting Shiva, one of the three main gods of Hinduism, with five faces, one of his manifestations. The Hindu divine trinity is formed by Brahma, Vishnu, and Shiva.

889

The Chitragupta temple
in Khajuraho (India), built in
the early eleventh century,
is dedicated to the Hindu god
Surya.

Bronze statuette
of the Hindu goddess
Sri-Devi, made in the
Chola period

890

("the city of the dead"), were built about
2500 BC. Surrounded by massive stone
walls, their streets were lined with two- and
three-room dwellings, some two or more stories high, built of dry stone. Many houses
had toilets. There was a city sewage system
made of earthenware pipes.

India was invaded for centuries (200 BC
to AD 500) by northern people, all of whom
had some effect on the development of
Hinduism. Its classical era is considered to
be between 320 and 480. It was then that the
great Hindu temples were built and much of
its ritual codified in the *Puranas* and *Sutras*.

The *Vedas*

The Hindu scriptures are called the *Vedas*,
from the Sanskrit word *Veda* for knowledge.
Considered *shruti* (what has been revealed
by the gods), they command the respect of

every Hindu. They record a tradition first transmitted orally for centuries by *rishis* (sages). Composed by the Indo-Aryans from c.2000–1700 BC and added to by the indigenous Dravidian people, they are not believed to have been written down until the third century BC. Also called the *Samhitas* (collection), the *Vedas* are four collections of hymns, poetry, and ceremonial incantations. The oldest is the *Rig-Veda*. *Rig* is Sanskrit for hymn. The work contains 1,028 hymns to a vast number of gods. The *Sama-Veda* (*sama* is the word for melody) is a hymnal. It draws verses from the *Rig-Veda* to be used by the *udgatri* (chanters). The *Yajur-Veda* (*yaja* is Sanskrit for sacrifice), consists of prose texts, proverbs, and prayers used in connection with offerings to the gods. The *Atharva Veda* is a compilation of magic spells.

The *Brahmanas* explain the hymns, their ritual uses, and their mythology. Supplementing the *Brahmanas* are the *Aranyakas*, the forest treatises, which date from the period between c.800 and 300 BC. The final section of them is called the *Upanishads* (c.600 BC), a philosophical work intended to teach the meaning of existence.

Hindu Literature
The *Mahabharata*

The *Mahabharata* and the *Ramayana* are epics. Considered *smriti* (what is remembered) rather than revealed, they are the stuff of story rather than theology, although their subjects are divinities.

The *Mahabharata* is principally concerned with the war between two groups of brothers, the Pandava, led by the god Krishna, and their cousins, the Kauravas. They are fighting over succession to the kingdom of the Bharatas, whose founder is the eponymous hero of India. The poem consists of some 200,000 lines, but the story of the war accounts for only half of them. Interwoven with it is a virtual encyclopedia of folklore, astronomy, law, geography, government, myths, and philosophy, frequently with no relationship to the main theme. These include the stories of Nala and Savitri, an abridged version of the *Ramayana*, and the *Bhagavad-Gita*.

The Bhagavad-Gita

Most scholars assume that the *Bhagavad-Gita* was written around 200 BC. Central to the worship of Krishna, this anonymous poem of 700 verses recounts the conversation between Krishna and his brother Arjuna just before the final conflict of the *Mahabharata* takes place. Krishna's urging of Arjuna to take action can be interpreted on

the philosophic level as advocating action rather than withdrawal from the world.

The Ramayana

The *Ramayana*, an epic of 50,000 lines, describes the efforts of Rama, king of Ayodhya, to recapture his wife, Sita, from the demon Ravana. Rama, less unpredictable

than Krishna, is one of the most popular divinities of Hinduism, honored in temples throughout India.

The Puranas

Both the eighteen great *Puranas* and the many subordinate *Puranas* were written after the epics and expand on some of their themes. They deal with a vast quantity of legendary and historical material about kings and cities, popular myths, and the ritual worship of Vishnu, Shiva, and other divinities.

The Sutras

The Dharmashastras and the *Dharmasutras*, part of the last works of the Vedic period called the *Sutras*, are discourses on religious practices, including marriage and funeral rites. Not venerated as *apaurusheya* (divinely inspired), they are nevertheless

Relief at Mamallapuram, one of the harbors of the Pallavas (a warrior dynasty of Hindu kings). It probably depicts the Ganges River falling onto the earth (on the left, with one leg lifted up), after a holy ascetic performed austerities for 1,000 years so that the gods would allow the river to bless the earth with its waters.

Relief depicting
one of the Hindu gods,
Shiva, slaying a demon. From
Khajurao, India

notable for their contribution to law.

Indo-Aryan Influence on Hinduism

Many of the precepts expressed in the *Vedas* are drawn from the native culture of the Indo-Aryans, which is related to that of the ancient Persians, Greeks, and Romans.

Indo-Aryan society was divided into social classes or castes. Although racism was not sanctioned in them, the *Vedas* distinguish *varnas* (colors) of people, probably originally to tell the lighter-skinned Indo-Aryan conquerors from the darker Dravidians. The word *varnas* was also used to define three classes, similar to those of Greco-Roman society. Based on occupation, these were the *Brahmans* or priests, the *Kshatriyas* or warriors, and the *Vaishyas* or tradespeople and farmers. Only after the Aryans settled in the Ganges Valley were the *Shudras*, or servants, defined as a fourth caste. Together the castes were said to form the body of the lord Brahma. Out of his mouth came the Brahmans; out of his arms, the warriors; out of his thighs, the tradespeople; and out of his feet, the servants. Ultimately, some 3,000 subcastes evolved.

Below the rungs of the caste ladder, outside the system of recognized castes, are millions of people, "outcastes" called the Untouchables. Traditionally ignored, they were regarded as unclean, like the work they typically performed. They cleaned the latrines and skinned the carcasses used for meat and leather. They were not allowed even to walk where the caste Hindus did, or to use the same wells or temples. In the twentieth century, the Indian leader Mahatma Gandhi called them the Children of God and performed the kinds of work traditionally assigned to them himself. Despite the fact that the caste system was officially abolished through his efforts by the first government of independent India, it still exists as a social phenomenon.

Svadharma

The caste system is supported by the Vedic philosophy of *svadharma* (personal *dharma*). It holds that the individual is born to a certain social level and occupation and should work within it to the best of his ability in order to fulfill his dharma (right social behavior). Caste traditionally determines the kind of food one eats. Only the *Shudras* are permitted meat. Hindu vegetarianism may well be based on practical considerations. Cows were regarded as sacred by the Indo-Europeans of the Persian heights, a concept passed on to Hinduism in the *Vedas*.

Religious Evolution

The *Upanishads* were composed about 600 BC, an era of radical change in the religious life of India. Various spiritual movements arose that interacted with Hinduism, Jainism, and Buddhism among them. These were characterized by a belief in *ahimsa* (nonviolence) and the cyclic nature of time.

Upanishad means to sit down near. It referred to this era when the sages ceased wandering in isolated seeking for truth and gathered their students to share the search. They did so in religious communities called *ashrams*.

The *Upanishads* present three interconnected concepts for the first time. The first is transmigration. The *atman* (soul) repeatedly dies and is reborn in a new organism, not necessarily human. (It could be in an animal or even a god.) The cycle of rebirth is called *samsara*.

The second concept is *karma*, the notion that people must bear the consequences of their deeds in their subsequent lives. Individuals were solely responsible for their destiny, through the choices made.

The final concept is that of *moksha* (release), the escape from the continuous cycle of death and rebirth to the final goal, *Nirvana* (literally, blow out, as in the flame of life). This is achieved with the union of the individual atman and the universal Brahman.

The *Vedas* stress works, sacrifice, and ritual; the carrying out of one's own dharma.

Statue from the south of India, carved in about the tenth century, depicting a Hindu goddess sitting in the meditative yoga posture

893

The *Upanishads* emphasize meditation and *sanatana dharma* (eternal dharma), transcending personal dharma. Sometime after 600, the religion of many north Indian people changed to one of *bhakti* (devotion).

Miniature from the seventeenth century, painted in Rajasthan, depicting the god Krishna and his beloved Radha

Ashramas (Stages of Life)

The older *Vedas* describe the obligations one is expected to meet in three stages of life: *brahmachari* (student); *grihasta* (householder), when one fulfills duties to spouse, family, and local community; and *vanaprastha* (hermit or denizen of the forest), who withdraws from material concerns to concentrate on religious matters and wider humanity. The *Upanishads* describe a fourth stage, that of the *sannyasin* (renouncer) who forswears all other obligations to focus on the passage to Nirvana.

The goals of human life are described in the older *Vedas* as *artha* (wealth or material success), *kama* (sensual pleasures), and *dharma* (right social behavior).

Hindu Deities

The *Vedas* discuss a central concept of god, that of Brahman, the god within and above all others (over 33 million of them). All other gods are considered but aspects of the One. Below and yet part of the Brahman, topping the pantheon of other deities, are Brahma the creator, Shiva the destroyer, and Vishnu the preserver of life. Shiva and Vishnu, like the other gods, are widely depicted in hundreds of forms, all part of rich Indian art, literature, music, and drama. Brahma, said to have been born from a lotus blossom that sprang from the navel of Vishnu, is considered to be above the level of popular worship. The others are widely venerated.

Vishnu

Vishnu is a gift-giving, benevolent god, the friend of all humankind. His followers are called Vaishnavas. He separated heaven and earth to create the universe and steps in often to save his handiwork. He comes to earth in the form of ten *avatars*. His first descent, or incarnation, was as the great fish Matsya, who helps Manu (the Noah of the Hindus) save the world from flood. Second, he became Kurma the turtle, who supports a mountain (Meru) used as a churn with which the gods stir up the milky cosmic ocean. Third, he appears as the boar Varaha, who slays a demon who had dragged the world to the depths of the cosmic ocean. Fourth, he becomes Narasimha, the demon-defeating man-lion. Fifth, he is the dwarf Vamana, who tricks the demon Bali into thinking he is a giant, stopping him from seizing the world. Vishnu's sixth manifestation is as Parashu Rama, a lumberjack who prevents the Kshatriyas from oppressing the Brahmans. Rama, hero of the *Ramayana*, is the seventh metamorphosis. Krishna, the eighth, is the incarnation described in the *Mahabharata*. On the ninth occasion, Vishnu becomes the historical Buddha himself. Finally the tenth and last appearance will be as Kalkin, the rider on a white horse, who will appear to destroy the universe and inaugurate a new

The Great Goddess (Devi) in her form as the terrifying Kali. In another manifestation she is Parvati, the beautiful wife of Shiva.

era when the present one collapses.

Hinduism posits the universe as a great sphere full of worlds, temporal and eternal, centered around the continent of India. It is cyclical in nature, repeatedly moving from a pure past (*Krita Yuga*) to the impure present (*Kali Yuga*), which deserves the fires and floods about to destroy it. A new pure era will then appear, beginning the cycle again.

Shiva

Shaivas, those who follow Shiva, believe he can create life as well as end it. He is the creator, destroyer, and repairer, the god of opposites, both benign and malevolent. Ending life in order to create new life, he is the god of reincarnation. He is venerated throughout India via the *lingam*, a stone monument representing the creative potentiality of life. Villagers bring flowers, rice, and fruit as symbolic offerings to the lingam in the local temples. Shiva is often worshiped as the four-handed dancing god Nataraja. As he dances on top of the dwarf of ignorance, his upper hands carry the fire of destruction and new life and the drum of time and creation. A raised right hand says, "Have no fear." His left hand points to the foot he has lifted as he steps out of the circle of fire that surrounds

Elaborate reliefs on the Jain Parshvanatha temple in Khajuraho, India, built in the eleventh century

Hindu relief of Shiva with his wife, Parvati (Uma-Maheshvara), from the seventh century

him, freeing himself from the eternal cycle of reincarnation.

Shiva is often portrayed with feminine aspects. He is usually depicted with a throat that is colored blue from drinking the sins of humankind. He often has a third eye, symbolizing higher consciousness, and a forehead bright with wisdom. His hair, frozen in the Himalayas, melts in the spring, letting the waters of the goddess Ganga flow.

Devi

Shiva's consort, Parvati, wakes him from a trance, freeing his powers. Daughter of the mountain Himalaya, she carries the creative ability of woman, called Shakti. Yet some say she is another aspect of Devi, who is presented in some stories as being in charge of the gods, ordering them to create or destroy. Bengalis worship her as Durga, the bringer of fall breezes, the rejoiner of families, and the destroyer of evil. As Kali, she can appear as the goddess of beauty or as a drinker of blood, reveling in animal sacrifice. Several goddesses may be aspects of her: Lakshmi, wife of Vishnu; Saravati, wife of Brahma; and Radha, wife of Krishna.

The Six Darshanas:
Philosophies of Hinduism

Six philosophical schools developed between 600 and 1800, part of a general trend toward religious questioning.

Karma Mimamsa

Mimamsa (inquiry) is the school of Vedic interpretation, and probably the most conservative school of Hinduism. It is a continuation of the Brahmanic theories of the importance of sacrifice and the influence of sound as the basis of the holy hymns and texts. The Vedas, said to have existed forever and assumed to continue into eternity, set therefore the highest standard.

Vedanta

Vedanta ("end of the Vedas") is the most important school of Hinduism and the core of traditional Hindu philosophy today. Rooted in the speculative treatises of the Aranyakas and the Upanishads, it has taken a number of different paths.

The great thinker Shankara (c. AD 788–

Stele from the first century AD depicting Durga, another aspect of the Great Goddess. She is carrying weapons, and stands on the head of the buffalo demon Mahisha.

The demon Rahu guards the entrance to a palace. Relief from Thailand, fifteenth century

A carved sandstone bracket from the gateway to a Buddhist stupa (reliquary mound), representing a tree goddess (Shalabhanjika), from the first or second century AD

820) believed in monism or nondualism, called *Advaita Vedanta*. He believed in the existence of Brahman as the divine absolute. The soul, although an aspect of Brahman, is prevented by *avidya* (ignorance) from understanding this. It does not realize that everything else in the outer world is but delusion created by *maya* (illusion). Through the knowledge given in the Vedanta, the soul gains proper understanding and thereby its salvation.

Ramanuja (who lived two centuries later and died in 1137) modified this thinking with a theory of qualified monism or nondualism, teaching that Brahman is the only reality, and everything, including the individual soul, is part of Brahman; that the soul can return to, but remain distinct from, Brahman.

Madhva, who lived in the thirteenth century (1199–1278), believed that the soul exists independent of a supreme being.

Vallabha (1479–1531) developed a system

The Hindu god Vishnu as Vishvarupa (Having All Forms), depicted as the whole world. Indian painting from Jaipur, early nineteenth century

This bronze statue of Jambhala, the Buddhist god of wealth, was made in Java, Indonesia, and dates from the ninth century. He is also worshiped by Hindus who call him Kubera.

a mental discipline, which ultimately leads to freedom from the bonds or toxins (*klesha*) that prevent a proper balance of spiritual energy by "yoking" the soul to the divine through these disciplines. The classic Yoga of Patanjali (c. second century BC) is regarded as the practical way to apply Sankhya.

Nyaya

Nyaya (analysis) emphasizes the effectiveness of knowledge as a means of achieving salvation. It also created a system of logic. By perception, deduction, comparison, and witnessing, true knowledge can be obtained.

Vaishesika

Vaishesika (school of individual characteristics) is closely related to Nyaya. It provides a list of the various forms into which reality can be classified and places emphasis on physics rather than theology. This philosophy holds the world is a composite of "atoms," which are distinct from the soul. Knowledge of these atoms produces freedom. The philosophy does not posit a supreme being.

Shakti/Devi

Toward the fifth century AD, a remarkable phenomenon appeared among the various Indian religious groups. This was the emergence of the worship of Shakti, or Devi, the Great Goddess, a combination of the Female Principle and the Mother Goddess, both traditions from pre-Aryan times.

This new religion attaches great importance to divine consorts. Mythologically, the Great Goddess was conceived as the bride of Shiva, and, like Shiva, she had both a peace-loving and a terrifying nature. From a philosophical point of view, the female deity represents the power or secret energy of the divine creative force. This vital force was called *shakti*; it formed the opposite pole of the male principle of consciousness and rest. Femaleness was associated with both matter and energy; maleness with the soul and passivity. The origin of this movement is probably to be found in the earlier philosophical school of Sankhya, in which the world is the result of the union between the material, or female, and the spiritual, or male.

Tantrism

Tantrism was developed in the sixth century on the basis of certain esoteric Hindu and Buddhist texts and rituals called *tantras* (meaning warp, or weaving). It is a pan-Indian belief with adherents in both Hinduism and Buddhism.

similar to that of Shankara, but with an emphasis on the grace of a personal god.

Sankhya

The Sankhya system, one of dualism, distinguishes between matter or nature (*prakriti*) and the soul (*purusha*). As in Jainism, the individual souls are seen as immortal and separate. Salvation lies in the restoration of the original perfect state of the immaterial soul. Sankhya is not concerned with the existence of a supreme being.

Yoga

Perhaps the oldest of the systems, Yoga (yoke) offers self-contained metaphysical theory, but adds to it the figure of Ishvara, a sublime god who has risen forever above the bonds of matter. Yoga is both a physical and

Early Chinese Thinkers

A Search for Peace and Order

Chinese terra-cotta
figure from
the seventh century BC
representing
a noble woman

During the late years of the Zhou (Chou) dynasty, despite the political turmoil (or because of it), several philosophies developed that would influence China's neighbors throughout eastern Asia. By 480 BC, the Zhou dynasty, which had once held a large part of China, no longer retained any real power. It performed only ceremonial functions. The country was politically fragmented. A number of independent principalities were incessantly in conflict. The ensuing period of chaos, from 480 BC to 221 BC, is known as the "the Warring Period."

Despite the many wars, Chinese civilization flourished. It was a time of great population growth, urban expansion, intensified agriculture, and economic development. The use of coined money and iron increased. Administration in the various states was restructured and the first laws codified in the second half of the fifth century BC. The army was reorganized, and the small force of aristocratic warriors replaced by a massive army of peasants.

China's constant warfare, with its resulting confusion and insecurity, fostered a search for peace and order in society and the state. During this period a number of philosophic schools formulated new ideas about the society. The most important of them was Confucianism, which ultimately became the central, universal philosophical tradition of China, Korea, Japan, and the northern part of southeast Asia. The written Chinese charac-

Bronze wire vessel
from the period of the Shang
(Chang) dynasty
(1766–1122 BC)

ter used for the word *classic* also means *warp*, the basis for weaving. The written threads of classical Chinese philosophy, called the Five Classics and the Four Books, were all created in this era, and Confucianism is woven through them all. They are *The Changes*, *The Writings of Old*, *The Poems*, *I li* (*The Ceremonials*), and *The Annals*; *Lunyu* (*The Sayings of Confucius*), *Mencius*, *The Doctrine of the Mean*, and *The Great Learning*.

Confucianism

Confucius (551–479 BC)

Confucius was born into the impoverished noble Kong (K'ung) family in 551 BC. His father was a minor bureaucrat in the feudal state of Lu, on the Shantung Peninsula. The philosophy of Confucius, a political thinker,

is rooted in his experience advising state leaders. His society granted him the title *Kong Fuzi* (*K'ung-fu-tzu*), or Grand Master Kong, which is *Confucius* in Latin, the name by which he is known in the West. Chinese society at that time was patriarchal and its organization feudal. Service to the government, not individual initiative, was sanctioned. Within the government, all records were maintained by a highly competitive literate elite, and the focus of all education was preparation for government work. Heaven (or the sky) was considered the great overseer that allowed the government to rule.

In a turbulent era Confucius sought order, internal and external, through personal right conduct and tradition, harking back to an ideal society exemplified in the early Zhou dynasty. He advocated reestablishing social order through a study of the rules of propriety outlined about five hundred years earlier in the Zhou literature. He saw the rulers of that period as meritorious leaders who had created an ideal society. At that earlier time, according to Confucius, people still knew the *Dao*, or right path. Study, especially the study of history, would help people to rediscover the *Dao* as a solution for the problems of a later time.

The *Lunyu* states, "Studying without thinking is wasted effort; thinking without studying is dangerous . . . those who have been born wise are the best people; then come those who have acquired wisdom by study; next are the ones who study to overcome their ignorance. Those who are ignorant and do not desire to study are the least of humankind . . . whoever has taken the *Dao* in the morning can die contented in the evening."

Although the entire *Lunyu* is traditionally attributed to Confucius, it is not certain which excerpts actually reflect his thinking, as opposed to that of his followers.

Confucius's thinking was original in its rationalism and humanism. He did not deny the existence of the supernatural, but he believed that an appeal to it made no sense: The primary focus, he contended, should be on individual effort.

"When the personal life is cultivated, the family will be regulated; when the family is regulated, the state will be in order; and when that state is in order, there will be peace throughout the world."

Confucius assumed a fundamental hierarchy in what he considered to be the five basic human relationships. Reflecting a patriarchal society, he considered the first relationship to be between ruler and subject; the second, between father and son; the third, between husband and wife; the fourth,

between an older and younger brother; and the fifth, between mutual friends. Confucius believed that of two friends, one always took the dominant role, and that those in authority in these relationships must never abuse the position. In the *Lunyu*, Zigong (Tsu Kong) asked: "Is there a single word that can serve as a guideline for life?" Confucius said: "Perhaps the word is reciprocity. Never do to another what you would not wish another to do to you . . . a human being who longs to occupy an important position helps another to such a position; one who wishes to succeed helps others to succeed. To judge others on the basis of what you know of yourself is the way to humanity . . . wealth and honor are what everyone desires, but if you can only obtain them by abandoning the right path, then it may be better for you not to have them."

An important tenet in the innovative teaching of Confucius was his interpretation

Decorations cast on the back of a Chinese bronze mirror from the end of the Zhou (Chou) dynasty (1122–c.221 BC)

903

Koung-Tsée, ou Confucius

A fantasy likeness of Confucius from eighteenth-century AD France

904

of the concept of nobility. Prior to him, nobility had been regarded in China as an inborn characteristic of aristocrats. But for Confucius, nobility meant a quality of the soul that could be acquired by study, by honesty, and by a virtuous life. "When a man departs from humanity, he no longer deserves the name." He attributed the misery of warfare in his lifetime to a lack of nobility on the part of the rulers, precisely the people who should have been setting a good example. When a prince behaved correctly, Confucius maintained, his subjects, from the highest to the lowest, would do so as well. His emphasis on secular human ethics was a new ideal for Chinese civilization.

Individuals, he said, should lead virtuous lives following the example set by their leaders. "He who exercises government by means of his virtue may be compared to the north polar star, which keeps its place and all the stars turn toward it."

Mencius (372–289 BC)

Confucius had many later followers and interpreters, the most important of whom was Meng K'o or Mengzi (Meng-zu). Like Confucius, he became well known in the West and his name was Latinized into Mencius. According to him, the restoration of unity to the empire would be the automatic consequence of a ruler's humanity and righteousness. He advocated humane government and rule by moral power. In a time when rulers were considered to be granted their positions by the Mandate of Heaven,

Bronze wire container from the beginning of the Shang (Chang) dynasty (1766–1122 BC)

Altar dedicated to Confucius in a temple in Taiwan

Mencius emphasized the duty of the ruler to the people. Believing people inherently good, he insisted that government be exercised on their behalf. When it was not, subjects had the right to depose it; if rebellion against a king occurred, it only indicated that heaven had withdrawn the mandate.

Mencius addresses King Hui of Liang State as follows: "If you, oh King, do not interrupt the normal course of farming by putting the farmers under arms, then there should be a surplus of grain. If fine-meshed nets are not used in fishing, there should be plenty of fish and turtles. If trees are cut at the right time, then there should be an inexhaustible quantity of wood. If the entire supply of grain, fish, and wood is not used, the result will be that the people can maintain the living and mourn the dead to their complete satisfaction. Maintenance of the living and mourning for the dead is the beginning of true kingship."

On another occasion the king is supposed to have asked Mencius what advantage these practices had to offer for his country. Mencius replied, "But why must you speak of advantage? It is always simply a question of humanity and doing your duty, that is all. When a king says: 'How can I benefit my country?' then the great people of the kingdom say: 'How can I benefit my family?' and the lower classes say: 'How can I benefit myself?' The state is imperiled while the classes fight with one another over benefits. . . . Let Your Majesty speak only of humanity and doing his duty."

Mencius assumed that human nature was originally good. He illustrates this with the

Pottery model of a Chinese house
from the period of the Han dynasty (207 BC–AD 220)

906

observation that if a person sees a child standing on the edge of a well, where he or she is in danger of falling in and drowning, that person will surely rush to save the child. It is only the circumstances in which people live that prevent this inherent goodness from constantly finding expression. Since moral power is inherent in everyone's nature, everyone can become a sage and all human beings are equal. Mencius believed that this equality gave the people the right to overthrow a wicked government.

Hsün-tzu, a contemporary disciple of Confucius, disagreed with Mencius. He contended that humans, who are by nature evil, require explicit controls to regulate their conduct. He did allow room for human improvement through education (by which he meant study of the classics of earlier societies) and social regulation. His views would be expanded into the philosophy of legalism.

The ideas of Confucius and Mencius, more idealistic than practical, were widely studied and discussed. But it was not until several centuries later, after Confucianism had undergone some necessary adjustments, that they began to exert a definitive influence

Chinese pottery group of four entertainers, found in a tomb from the Han dynasty

Glazed ceramic in the shape of a barking dog, from the Han dynasty

907

An audience at
the court of one of the
Han emperors.
Illustration from the eighteenth
century AD

on political ideology. The Confucians were not interested so much in politics as in the practice of ritual, a topic of many old Confucian texts. Correct performance had a magic significance for the Confucians: It was believed that if a ruler performed the proper ritual, or had it performed, then a peacemaking process would automatically be set in motion.

It appears that only a few of Confucius's followers managed to obtain positions in the government, and those with government appointments were frequently the objects of mild ridicule. The Confucians were not purely political thinkers, but also "masters of ceremonies," criticized by rival schools for their love of rituals and what was considered their uselessness to society. Confucianism thus did not become an official state ideology without a struggle. It had first to deal with the competition of a group that offered more practical solutions, namely the school of legalism. Over the short term the legalist had greater success.

Legends about Laozi

It is not certain that Laozi (Lao-tzu), the "Old Master" of Daoism (Taoism), was ever actually a living person, yet a great many legends have been created about him. A story is told that his mother was a virgin who carried him in her womb for eighty years, and his father was a beam of sunlight. It was therefore not surprising to hear that on the day he was born little Laozi was as learned as a sage of eighty, his hair already gray.

Laozi is said to have held a position as record keeper for the Zhou Empire, and to have been the teacher of Confucius. The Daoists like to say that Confucius was his worst pupil. Zhuangzi (Chuang-tzu) says that Confucius sought out Laozi and wanted to talk with him about humanity and duty. Laozi said: "Seagulls do not become white by washing themselves every day; crows do not become black by dipping themselves daily in ink. In these cases, black and white are natural characteristics, so it cannot be said that one is better than the other. One who understands the *Dao* and employs humanity and duty to distinguish between good and evil is making the same mistake."

According to legend, Laozi, disgusted with the conditions of society in his time, simply rode off one day on a buffalo to the far West. Shortly before leaving China, he recorded his ideas for posterity in *The 5,000 Words*, the *Daode Jing* (*Tao-te Ching*). He handed over the book to a border guard, telling him to take good care of it and, mounted on his buffalo, left China forever. Some say that he went to India, where he taught the Indians a modified version of his theories, which came to be known as Buddhism.

Laozi (Lao-tzu) on his buffalo, on his way to the West, holding in his hand the scroll of *Daode Jing*. Statuette from the Han dynasty

Legalism

Legalism was a rationalist philosophy of government. Whatever the ruler did to promote the power of the state and the army was thought of as justified. Legalism insisted that pragmatic, not virtuous or humanistic, considerations dictate government actions. Legalism's motto was, 'Make the state rich and the army strong." The authority of the ruler and his administrative apparatus had to be absolute, with people kept in check by a rigidly applied system of punishments and rewards that was established through detailed legislation. Legalism assumed that

An bronze plate
from the first century BC,
depicting a tiger attacking an
ibex

strict enforcement of regulations, with specific penalties for violations, would result in the efficient management of society. It led to a government that was permitted unlimited rule that became the dominant philosophy of the next dynasty, the totalitarian Qin (Ch'in).

In 221 BC the northwestern feudal state of Qin succeeded to the royal power that Chinese states had warred over since 500 BC. Its king, advised by the prominent legalistic philosopher Shang Yang (c.390–338 BC), declared himself *Shih Huang Ti*, or First Emperor of the Qin dynasty. The name *China*, describing the entire country, would be adopted by the rest of the world.

Two other outstanding legalists, Li Su (280–208 BC) and Han Feizi (d. 233 BC), councilors to the first emperor, expanded the views of Hsün-tzu, putting their emphasis on control of human nature and the punishment of antisocial behavior. They subordinated personal freedom to authority. Han Feizi wrote: "We must not listen to those who argue on behalf of humanity and duty, because if they are heeded, nothing practical

will any longer be achieved. Also, those who apply themselves to culture and scholarship must not be taken into the service, because, if they are, they impede the application of the law. . . . Since the interests of the ruler and the subject differ in this manner, it is impossible for the ruler to approve the deeds of an individual and at the same time to promote the welfare of the state."

The Qin administration mandated uniformity in order to promote the economic and social integration of the vast empire. It standardized coinage, weights and measures, axle widths—and culture. It simplified character writing, developing the Simple Seal system and making its use compulsory. The emperor also attempted to standardize thinking. In 213 BC he made legalism the state doctrine and ordered the books of all other philosophies burned.

The legalists made an important contribution in their concept of government as an independent entity that transcended the whim of any particular ruler, and in their creation of an administrative apparatus that could function autonomously. In 206 BC a rebel army officer proclaimed the new Han dynasty. It would retain the centralized system of state administration of the Qin, but would reject most other aspects of legalism. (The Qin-style hierarchy of administration lasted until 1912.) The new Han government turned to Confucianism as the underlying philosophy of the vast bureaucracy it utilized to organize and control its empire.

Daoism (Taoism)
Lao-tzu (c.570–c.490 BC)

The sage Laozi (Lao-tzu—"the Old Master"), a contemporary of Confucius, sought Dao (the Way) in nature rather than society. He examined nature to understand humanity, focusing on personal growth rather than communal. The *Tao-te Ching* (*Classic of the Way of Power*), explaining his philosophy, is attributed to him by tradition, although it may have been recorded by his students from things he said. In it, people are asked to go with the flow of nature, a philosophy of nonaction called *wu-wei*. Laozi emphasized a return to simple agrarian life, one not regulated by government. He rejected both the pragmatism of the legalists and the moralizing of the Confucians. His ideal was to let things take their course, not to try to think and do what is right, but to think and do nothing: "the doing of non-doing." The Tao of Taoism is a metaphysical-individualistic concept, as opposed to the Tao of Confucianism, which offers a social ideal.

The *Daode Jing*, the oldest and most important document in this religion, is attrib-

uted to Laozi. It says: "When the best kind of people learn the Way, then they are able, with dedication, to put it into practice. When average people are told of the Way, they can retain some things, but they forget the others. When the lowest kind of people hear of the Way, they laugh loudly at it. If they do not laugh at it, then it cannot be the Way. The proverb therefore goes as follows: The light Way seems dark; the Way that goes forward seems to lead backward; the smooth Way seems rough; the highest virtue is as low as a valley; the purest white seems dirty; enormous virtue seems inadequate; resolute virtue seems small and weak; the simplest reality seems to change. The great square has no corners, the great cask takes much time to make, the great sound makes little noise, the great image has no form. The Way is glorious, but has no name. Only the Way is good in beginning things and good in bringing things to an end. . . . Those who study hard increase every day. Those who have under-stood the Way decrease every day. They decrease and decrease until they reach the point where they do nothing. They do nothing, and yet nothing remains undone. When someone wishes to rule the world, he must be detached, because if he is drawn to objects he will be unfit to rule the world."

Zhuangzi (c.369–286 BC)

A subsequent important proponent of Taoism was Zhuangzi. He used the *Tao-te Ching* as a starting point, reinterpreting its abstract ideas in more accessible colloquial language. His work, the *Chuang-tzu*, is characterized by an objective humor that made it popular even with the Confucians he frequently ridiculed.

Later Developments

Under the Han dynasty (207 BC–AD 220) the Confucianist ethic was adopted to restore the social order and rationalize the system of power, and was combined with ancient

Model of a boat and crew from a Han dynasty tomb (AD 25–220)

911

Bronze horse
with one foot resting
on a swallow, from
the Han dynasty

Expansion of Confucianism and Taoism

Influence of Confucianism and Taoism

The Spread of
Confucianism and
Taoism

Chinese ideas of the cosmos. It was deemed insufficient for rulers merely to exercise power; they had to legitimize it by determining the will of heaven. The old idea of the Mandate of Heaven regained its importance. The emperor was called the Son of Heaven, and approval or disapproval of his administration was registered by natural phenomena. Heaven was thought to be able to withdraw its approval from the actions of a wicked prince and transfer the mandate of government to someone more worthy.

The Han emperors adopted Confucianism in 136 BC, as well as the Confucian principle of appointing officials on the basis of merit. They expanded the bureaucracy to meet the needs of more people. They used the administrative apparatus set up by the Qin dynasty but modified many of its policies. They required written examinations to find qualified people, rather than handing out offices on the basis of birth or personal connection. They required the study of Confucianism for government service, establishing an official academy for public administrators in 124 BC, based on the Five Classics.

This was also a period of fusion. Taoist Confucianism emphasized the cultivation of just moral behavior through retreats; legalistic Confucians argued for strict, impartial observance of the law, to put an end to arbitrary power. "Orthodox" Confucianism continued to exist as an intricate system of ritual formulas. In the third century AD, Confucianism underwent a complete reinterpretation based on the oracular *Yi Jing* (*I Ching*), the *Daode Jing*, and the works of Zhuangzi. A speculative attitude developed that reflected the desire for individualism and personal salvation.

Confucianism had religious competition in Buddhism and Daoism. Mahayana Buddhism, known in China since the first century AD, reached the court by the fourth century. Its concepts fit in easily with the metaphysical speculation of Confucianism and with the rise of a religious Daoism that evolved from several sectarian movements. It posited a pantheon of supernatural forces, the possibility of corporal immortality, and personal liberation. In the ninth century, Buddhists in China were persecuted by a government that attacked it as an alien element whose temples had become too powerful. The decline of Buddhism meant a corresponding increase in Daoism, which became the dominant factor in Chinese religious life. Starting with the Tang dynasty (AD 618–907), Confucianism again became the guiding doctrine of the intellectual upper class. The teachers of the texts used to train public officials were Confucians after all, and only those who had mastered the texts could hold office.

Part of one of the so-called Dead Sea scrolls. These scrolls, probably written by the Essenes, contain writings from the Old Testament and were found in Qumran.

The Jewish People

Unification, Captivity, and Revolt

After the death of King Solomon in 922 BC, popular dissension among the Israelites over his rule led to the division of his kingdom into two others. Ten of the original twelve Hebrew tribes established the kingdom of Israel in the north. Two (the tribes of Benjamin and Judah) remained in the south with Rehoboam, in the kingdom of Judah.

Israel, under its king Omri (who reigned from 876–869 BC), dominated not only Judah but their rival kingdoms Moab, Edom, and Damascus. Omri made Samaria his capital in 870 BC. His son and successor, Ahab, married the pagan Jezebel, setting off a religious battle as she tried to add her Phoenician god to Israel's monotheism. When the

913

The valley
of the River Jordan

Assyrian Tiglath-Pileser III captured the entire region in 734 BC, Samaria held out until 721 BC. The Assyrians drove the northern "Lost Tribes" of Israel into exile and subjugated the Hebrews of Judah. They brought Mesopotamian colonists into Samaria who took up the religious practices of the Israelites, forming the Samaritan sect.

Retaining their own identity over the next century, the Jews in Judah objected to the takeover of regional power by the Chaldean Empire of Babylonia. In 598 BC, its king Nebuchadnezzar II seized Jerusalem and deported the Jewish elite to Babylon in order to break down ethnic resistance.

He allowed Zedekiah, of the lineage of David, to rule the remnants of Judah. A decade later, Zedekiah revolted. Over the next two years, the Chaldeans razed the country, destroying Jerusalem in 596 BC. They sent the last potentially rebellious Jews to join the others in Babylon, leaving only scattered peasants in Judah. A group of refugees fled to Egypt with their reluctant prophet Jeremiah.

Babylonian Captivity (586–516 BC)

The exiles from Judah found a vibrant community of Jews in Babylon, some of whom had fled there from Israel over a century earlier. Under the guidance of Ezekial and a prophet called Deutero-Isaiah, they not only maintained their identity against what they saw as insidious pagan influences, they developed their religion. They ritualized their prayer services and fashioned the records of Yahweh's people into the beginnings of the Bible. They made converts and many of them put down roots in Babylonia, but they still cherished hope of returning. They had the right, they thought, to dwell in the land given them by God and to worship in their Temple.

Return to Jerusalem

Babylon was conquered by Cyrus the Great, the founder of the Persian Empire, in 539 BC. A year later he liberated the Jews by edict, encouraging their return to their homeland to the point, it is said, of contributing money to the cause himself.

914

The Davidic prince Zerubbabel departed from Babylon in 536 BC, accompanied by 42,000 Jews bearing only whatever possessions they could carry. They found Palestine still showing the effects of war and their own presence resented by the indigenous inhabitants, particularly the Samaritans. Cyrus's successors continued his liberal policy with regard to the Jews. In conflicts with their neighbors, Jerusalem's colonists could generally rely on support from the authorities in Persepolis. However, rebuilding both the

Miniature from a Pentateuch of the seventh century BC that is kept in Tours, France, showing the god Yahweh committing himself to the people of Israel on Mount Sinai

915

country and the Temple was a daunting prospect. The prophets Haggai and Zechariah encouraged them and by 516 BC, a date traditionally seen as the end of the Babylonian captivity, they had rebuilt the

Jerusalem insufficiently orthodox and set about instituting religious reform. However, it is unlikely that he could have achieved his goal without the help of Nehemiah, who arrived thirteen years later with another group of immigrants.

Nehemiah was not a scholar but a man of importance who had been a favorite cup-bearer at the court of Artaxerxes I, king of Persia from 465 to 425 BC. He brought with him documents that specified the rights of the Jews with respect to the *satrap* of Samaria, assuring the Jews of virtual autonomy. While Ezra carried out his religious reforms, Nehemiah directed the reconstruction of Jerusalem and the civil administration of Judaea. Together they read the Torah, the books of the Law, aloud to the people. These books, containing 1,521 prohibitions and

Jewish religion is characterized by the many daily regulations and directions that are described in the Torah. This photograph shows a little room that was specially built for ritual cleansing, in a twelfth-century AD house in Gerona.

Second Temple. It was smaller than Solomon's great edifice, but Yahweh again had a home. His people elected the Jewish high priest as ruler, establishing Judah (or Judaea) as a theocracy.

In Babylon the glad tidings were received with great acclaim. New migrations took place. In 457 BC the priest Ezra led 1,800 of the faithful to Jerusalem. He was a formidable expert in the Law who claimed descent from Aaron. He considered the Jews in

A silver *besomnibus* decorated with jewels. At the *hawdala* (end of sabbath) all members of a Jewish family take a sniff from the herbs (*bessamin*) that are kept in this container in order to drive away the sadness caused by the end of the sabbath.

regulations, governed all parts of their lives. The people assembled in a valley outside the city, and took five oaths. They swore to obey the law of Moses, not to associate with the pagans, and to observe the Sabbath, doing no business and cultivating no land that day. (Ezra and Nehemiah did allow the Jews to give their seventh day, the day of rest, a touch of festivity.) They swore to give alms to the Temple, contributing tithes (a tenth of their income) and the firstborn of their cattle. The Jews ate only meat that had been ritually slaughtered. They refused some food altogether, including pork, hare, celery, and shellfish.

Diaspora

The Jews remained subjects of the Persian Empire, despite their theocracy. In 331 BC Alexander the Great of Macedonia conquered Persia, making Judaea an imperial province. He adopted the Persian policy of special privilege for the Jews, encouraging thousands of them to emigrate to Alexandria after he made it his capital. Thousands more emigrated throughout the known world, as commerce improved under the united empire, especially Greece. Their migration was called *diaspora* (dispersion in Greek).

Hellenism

Alexander's empire was divided among his generals after his death in 323 BC. Ptolemy I was made king of Egypt, where he reigned from 323 to 285 BC. He invaded and occupied Palestine, strategically located on the trade route to Arabia.

Legend has it that his son, Ptolemy II, called Philadelphus (brotherly), a great patron of art and learning, sent a letter to Eleazar, the high priest of Jerusalem, with a request for translators to render the Hebrew Bible into Greek. Eleazar sent seventy-two scholars, six from each tribe, to Alexandria. Working independently of each other in separate cells, they arrived at identical translations. This was named the Septuagint, from *septuaginta* (seventy), after the seventy-two scholars. (It is customarily abbreviated LXX, the Roman numerals for seventy.)

Far from their roots, the Jews of Greece adopted not only the language but the customs of the Greeks in an adaptation of Hellenism that would come to vie with Judaism itself. In 198 BC Syria's ambitious king Antiochus III (the Great) conquered the possessions of Egypt's king Ptolemy V in Palestine and Lebanon. At first it seemed that the change of master would have little consequence for the Jews, despite the new king's emphasis on Hellenism. The upper classes in Palestine, eager to advance in

society, had little objection to Hellenism. Prominent Jews, even high priests, took Greek names. But the common people preferred the old traditions and had no interest in Greek culture. They began to take an increasingly militant attitude toward the collaborators. A movement of orthodox Jews

The city of Masada lay high on a plateau in the mountains near the Dead Sea. Masada was the last refuge of Jewish Zealots after the Romans conquered Jerusalem in AD 70.

917

arose who were concerned with living according to the Law.

But Antiochus IV, called Epiphanes (the Illustrious), who succeeded his father in 175 BC, seized Jerusalem in 168 BC and outlawed Judaism. He then attempted to mandate the worship of Greek gods. Hellenistic Jews assisted him. They had taken possession of the Temple and appointed a high priest named Jason. He built a Greek gymnasium, where young men trained in the nude, their loyalty evident by their opposition to circumcision. Some of them sent a representative to the pagan games in honor of Heracles. Yet it was one of Jason s own party

Close-up of the ruins of Masada. When the Romans broke through its defense, the Zealots committed suicide.

who finally drove him from power.

This man, Menelaus, persuaded King Antiochus to appoint him as high priest replacing Jason, promising that he would get four hundred more talents (approximately 3,000 shekels) from the Jews each year. When the Jews did not agree, he let the Temple treasury be plundered. When the uproar this caused was reported to the king in 167 BC, he ordered the people of Jerusalem to bring offerings to the pagan gods. He ordered those killed who refused.

The Hasmonaeans (Maccabees)

In the town of Modein, where Hellenization was well under way, a Syrian officer assembled the people around a hastily erected altar and ordered the citizens to perform sacrifice. According to legend, the Jewish priest Mattathias, head of the Hasmonaean dynasty, refused. Then another Jew stepped forward and made his offering. Beside himself with rage, Mattathias struck down the collaborator and the Syrian officer. That day there were no sacrifices in Modein. But Mattathias realized that he must go into hiding. With his five sons he withdrew into the desert, where he organized a guerrilla army known to history as the Maccabees. The Syrian military power was ineffective against its guerrilla tactics. When the old leader died, his sons buried him in the family tomb outside Modein.

According to a *New York Times* article (November 18, 1995), this grave has probably been discovered (on November 15, 1995). A mechanical excavator expanding a highway in modern Modein, near Jerusalem, dug into a man-made burial cave. Twenty-three ossuaries (containers of bones) were discovered, one with the ancient Hebrew letters *HASM...*, presumably for Hasmonaean. Many of the ossuaries were inscribed in Greek (names like Sara, Mariama, Elizier), as would be expected from the Hellenism of the era. The name *Shimon* was in Hebrew. Efrat Auerbach of the Israeli Antiquities Authority said she believed the find to be a family tomb used between the first century BC and the first century AD.

Mattathias's son Judas took over the leadership, continuing the rebellion against the degenerating Seleucid kingdom. In its capital, Antioch, one usurper followed on the heels of another. The Jewish leader took full advantage of the situation, mobilizing popular support against the Syrians. He was killed in battle, fighting a much larger Syrian army with only eight hundred followers. His example inspired the Jews. His brothers, like their father, Mattathias, began again from the wilderness and radicalized the entire people. While Mattathias had asked for little more than the freedom to live as an orthodox Jew, his sons demanded political autonomy and, ultimately, independence. The Maccabees conquered Jerusalem in 164 BC. Their rededication of the Temple is commemorated by the festival of Hanukkah. The kings of Syria were forced to acknowledge that they were unable to rule Palestine, part of Phoenicia, and some areas across the Jordan. They let themselves be bought off for three hundred gold talents. (In 138 BC, Judas's brother Simon minted the first Jewish coins. They bore a palm frond and the inscription *Holy Jerusalem*.)

The Maccabees established the Sanhedrin, a state council of seventy-one priests and religious leaders responsible for all religious and civil legal matters. New political parties grew out of religious and political differences. The two most important were the

Sadducees and the Pharisees.

The Sadducees (or Zadokites) took their name from Zadok, a priest under Kings David and Solomon (see the Old Testament, 2 Samuel 15:24–29). A party of aristocrats, they drew sponsorship from the clerical elite ousted by the Maccabees. They accepted

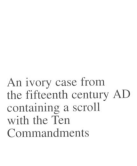

An ivory case from the fifteenth century AD containing a scroll with the Ten Commandments

Crystal lamp from the seventeenth century AD decorated with texts from the Torah written in Hebrew, from the synagogue in Damas

919

only the written Torah as binding law, rejecting all other interpretations, especially those of the Pharisees. They did not believe in personal immortality or the existence of angels, specifically rejecting those concepts being preached at the time by Jesus. The day the Sanhedrin abrogated their legal code was made a holiday.

The Pharisees, formed in the second cen-

Silver Torah shield with a decorative crown on which the Ten Commandments are written. This shield comes from a nineteenth-century AD synagogue in Italy.

tury BC as the Hasidim, rigidly observed the written law but also accepted the validity of the oral law that had developed as scholars strove to interpret tradition. Partly because of their rejection of Hellenism, they gained many adherents among the common people. Postulating an ethical and spiritual form of Judaism, they would survive the destruction of the Temple in AD 70 and go on to lead the dispersed Jews. The Sadducees would fade from history. Meanwhile, the ongoing conflict between the Pharisees and the Sadducees weakened the Jews and gave foreigners an opportunity for aggression and influence.

Under the rule of the high priest John Hyrcanus, the state took over Samaria and Edom (or Idumaea), coercing their people into converting to Judaism. His sons Hyrcanus II and Aristobulus II competed for succession to the throne of Judaea. The Edomite (or Idumaean) Antipater, an apparent supporter of Hyrcanus, plotted with the Roman emperor Pompey the Great to intervene on his own behalf. In 62 BC the Roman army seized Jerusalem and made the kingdom of Judaea a client state. In 47 BC Judaea was made directly subject to the empire. Antipater was appointed procurator. His son Herod the Great was crowned king of Judaea in 37 BC.

Herod (73–4 BC)

The foreigner Herod the Edomite emerged from the welter of first-century BC political politics as the strongest man in Palestine. The support that he gave the Roman Augustus secured him not only great power, but a royal scepter. From 25 to 4 BC Augustus supported Herod because Herod was loyal to him. As a foreigner's son, King Herod the Great was automatically regarded as godless. He could expect nothing from the Pharisees, with their emphasis on protecting Judaism from outside influence, so he supported the opposing Sadducees, despite the fact that he cared nothing for Jewish Law. He conducted a reign of terror even among the members of his family. His wife knew that she would be killed upon his death. Every high official understood that his life depended on the king's whim.

Herod's unpopularity was due in no small part to economic depression. He lived in great luxury in a country wasted by wars. He had magnificent buildings built in his own honor. He even rebuilt the Temple in Jerusalem until it surpassed Solomon's in size, but the golden eagle on the gate was a reminder of his own power. The masses grew impoverished as taxes to pay for his projects rose to unbearable levels. Farmland was concentrated in the hands of a very few. Believing a divided population easier to rule, he brought many Gentiles into the country. He expanded the Greek settlement of Straton's Tower into the great city of Caesarea and gave both Jews and Gentiles the rights of citizens. He liked to stay there to escape the orthodox atmosphere of Jerusalem. Caesarea was a sophisticated city, with temples and amphitheaters. The king developed it into a major trading center, the leading city in southern Syria. The Roman soldiers who supported him as king were quartered there, although there was also a cohort in

Jerusalem. The Antonia fortress, built at the corner of the temple, commanded the forecourts. When the Jewish temple police could not control riots, the Roman legionaries would intervene.

Roman Rule

Herod died in 4 BC. The matter of his succession was decided at the imperial court in Rome. Augustus heard the arguments of three claimants, sons of Herod, and received a Jewish embassy, which requested that Palestine be made an independent province. In the end he divided the kingdom. Archelaus, the cruel and incompetent eldest son, was given the coastal area; his brother, the foolish Herod Antipas, got the region around Lake Tiberias; and the moderate and decent Philip was allowed to rule in Transjordan.

The unpopular Archelaus had to battle to retain his throne. After ten years of misrule, Jews and Samaritans filed a complaint against him with Augustus. The Roman *princeps* was persuaded and removed Archelaus, setting his kingdom under the authority of the governor of Syria. However, he also

A parchment scroll from the eighteenth century AD containing the handwritten texts of the Torah

A Jewish coin from the time when the Maccabeans defeated the Syrians and conquered Jerusalem

Remains of the synagogue that was built in Capernaum (Tell Choem) in the second century AD

A seder plate from the nineteenth century AD that was used at the celebration of Passover

gave Judaea a procurator of its own, who supervised provincial administration from Caesarea. Most other matters were dealt with by the Sanhedrin, the temple council in Jerusalem. The common people were no better off than before. The crisis continued; the faithful were frustrated by their subjection to a Gentile. Social demands were intermingled with religious. The Pharisees, still trying to preserve Jewish identity within the existing order, achieved a measure of official recognition. No longer considered a threat to the ruling classes, they even saw high priests adopt their beliefs on occasion.

A new party was formed that objected to any Jewish acquiescence to Roman authority. The members called themselves Zealots.

The Zealots

The Zealots advocated actual revolt against the Romans. The Roman government outlawed them and imposed ever tighter restrictions on them. They never gained the support of the majority of people. The average Jew may have sympathized with their actions, but did not dare offer them active support. In general the masses adhered to the collaborative wisdom of the Pharisees.

In AD 66 the Zealots initiated a rebellion against Rome. Many of the Zealots adopted urban guerrilla tactics, seizing power in Jerusalem. During the street battles, a number of buildings caught fire. One of them was the office of the city notary, where all the debt records were kept. Roman control went

סימן סכום כסרי סימא נסטה

Jewish religion emphasizes reading of the Torah. This illustration from the sixteenth century AD shows a Jewish school in the Middle Ages.

up in flames with the papers.

The Roman emperor Nero sent in General Vespasian (later emperor) to reassert imperial authority. He conducted a war of extermination, but his legions restored order. In AD 70 they recaptured and razed Jerusalem, destroying the Temple forever by the order of Titus, the emperor from AD 79 to 81.

Masada
A thousand Zealots withdrew to the historic mountaintop named Masada, in southern

Israel. Jews had used it as a fortress since ancient times. The besieged Zealots held off the Romans for two years. When the Romans finally defeated them in AD 73, all but three of the Zealots committed suicide.

Part of the Wailing Wall that once formed the eastern wall of the Temple of Jerusalem. Jews come here to mourn the Temple's destruction by the Romans in AD 70.

An illustrated scroll in a silver case from the eighteenth century AD that contains the Book of Esther

Christianity

The Beginning

As the first millennium AD opened, some eight million Jews faced religious and political ferment within Judaism and long-simmering conflict with Hellenism, originated by Alexander the Great to impose unity on the diverse cultures of his empire. Their state, Judaea, was locally ruled by the Edomite king Herod Antipas and was part of the Roman Empire under Caesar Augustus. Their people had been dominated before by Egypt, Assyria, Babylonia, Persia, and Greece. Their scriptures told of a savior called the Messiah who would free them from bondage. The man named Jesus was born into this culture sometime between 8 and 4 BC, according to most scholars today. (The Gregorian calendar, introduced in 1592, used this date to define *Anno domini* [the year of the lord.]) The name *Jesus* is the Greek version of the Hebrew *Joshua*, which means "Jehovah is salvation."

His father was a carpenter in Nazareth, a small village in the northern Palestinian region of Galilee. What is known about him comes from the Gospels, the first four books of the New Testament of the Bible. These were written some fifty years after his death in AD 30 or 31. (The other books detail the

Miniature from a French manuscript from the thirteenth century. It shows scenes from the life of John the Baptist. Above he is preaching and below he performs a baptism. Though he historically baptized in the River Jordan, this shows the newly baptized in a wooden tub in a medieval church while men made ugly by their lechery peer through the window.

beliefs of the early Christians.) Only Matthew and Luke give the story of Jesus' birth in Bethlehem. They describe his mother, Mary, as a virgin and his father as the God of the Jews. They tell of his humble birth in a manger, yet of a visit by three kings guided by a special star. This dual emphasis on his humility and nobility, like his descent from Abraham and David, is basic to Christianity. Jesus' education in Judaic traditions is emphasized in the story in Luke about his confounding the Temple elders in Jerusalem with his knowledge of the scriptures at age twelve.

Baptism

According to Luke, John the Baptist was Jesus' second cousin. He chose to spend his life in solitude in the desert, appearing at intervals on the banks of the Jordan River to preach. John brought people hope, announcing that the kingdom of God was at hand, that he had been sent to prepare the way. John baptized his followers to wash away the sins of their former ways of life (Mark 1:4). "All the land of Judaea were baptized of him in the river of Jordan" (Mark 1:5). Such ritual cleansing was part of Jewish law (Leviticus 11:25, 40, 15:5–7). Ezekial 36:25 refers to Jews being cleaned by water from the Jordan prior to the establishment of the kingdom of God. King Herod sent spies to ascertain the nature of the gatherings. Past revivalist movements had frequently led to uprisings. "Let him who has two sets of garments give one to him who has none, and with food, let it be the same," taught John (Luke 3:11). Herod, who taxed his subjects heavily, might have wondered at the implications of this. Mark 1:9–11 describes John baptizing Jesus. Baptism became the initiation rite of Christianity (Acts 2:3).

After baptism, Jesus withdrew for "forty days," a time when he was symbolically tempted to forgo his mission (Matthew 4:8). He then took up his public ministry. Meanwhile, John had fallen into serious trouble. In his preaching, he had emphasized Herod's scandalous life, particularly his sexual escapades. The king had the prophet imprisoned and subsequently executed.

The Preaching of Jesus

While John was still in prison, Jesus began to preach. In contrast to the prophet, Jesus was not an ascetic nor did he advocate asceticism. His message seems to have defied all the conventional systems. There was none of the strict dogma of the Pharisees or the legalism of the Zealots. Jesus was uncompromising in his view that it was not the letter of the Law that mattered, but the spirit. He drew on the concept of Rabbi Hillel: "Do not do to another what you would not wish to be done to you." But Jesus put the same idea in a positive form: "Love your neighbor as your-

self." He objected to the notion of religious exclusivity, for neighborly love implied respect for other people. The area where he had grown up, the "Galilee of the Gentiles," as it was called in the scriptures, had been settled by Jews and non-Jews (Gentiles) alike. Syrians, Greeks, and Romans added their languages to the Semitic Aramaic Jesus and his fellow Jews spoke. He was familiar with many cultures and insisted that his message excluded no one. He took meals with "publicans and sinners," preached to "the lost sheep of Israel," did not condemn an adulteress or a Jew (Zacchaeus) who collected Roman taxes from his own people. Miracles and healings, according to the Gospels, gave power to his words. With them, he cured people of illnesses popularly considered the consequence of sin.

"When you prepare a midday or evening meal," Jesus taught, "do not invite your friends or your brother or your relatives or your rich neighbors who would be able to invite you in their turn, so that you would receive repayment. But when you prepare a feast, invite the beggars, the misshapen, the lame, and the blind. And you shall receive payment, although they have nothing with which to pay you. For you shall be repaid upon the rising of the righteous" (Luke 14:12–14). Jewish leaders of the day considered this eating with the "unclean" a violation of religious law, and the Roman government was also threatened.

Disciples
His preaching attracted all kinds of people. The Gospels tell of twelve disciples, symbolic of the twelve tribes of Israel. He called them from normal occupations, again a

Mosaic in the Church of Sant' Apollinare in Ravenna, showing Christ meeting his future disciples Simon and Andrew. Simon was later called Peter.

927

Byzantine fresco from the sixteenth century in one of the Meteorite monasteries in Greece. It depicts Christ attending a wedding in Canaan, where he was said to have turned water into wine.

reflection that his message was universal, for everyone, not just a priestly elite. Jesus mercilessly attacked religious hypocrisy and exploitation. This brought him more followers. The popularity of Jesus was a direct threat to the religious establishment. The Pharisees felt that only "by the prince of devils casteth he out devils" (Mark 3:22). They also objected to the fact that his disciples harvested grain on a day meant to be sacred to the Lord. Jesus responded: "The Sabbath was made for man, not man for the Sabbath; . . . the Son of Man is Lord of the Sabbath" (Mark 2:27–28).

Messiah

Still more threatening was the idea that Jesus might be the Messiah. People responded to Jesus' miracles by beginning to regard him as the promised savior. The Jews believed that their savior must be a king, a man who could free them from political subjugation.

Byzantine painting
from the sixteenth century:
Christ enters Jerusalem
in a triumph.

928

EHGIPTI SIMVLACRA FVGVAT PRECENCIA XPI:

His followers clearly regarded Jesus originally as a temporal ruler. They called him "Messiah" or "Anointed," a name used for the king in the time of David, and a threat to Herod.

Jesus preached for perhaps only a year, certainly no more than three, before traveling to Jerusalem. It was Passover time. Thousands of Jews went to the city to celebrate the Jewish deliverance from Egypt. The Roman procurator Pontius Pilate had also sought lodgings in Jerusalem. Jesus entered the city, not on a spirited horse as would have befitted a rival to Herod, but riding a donkey. According to the prophecy of Zechariah, "The king cometh unto thee . . .

Ivory panel from the thirteenth century depicting the Holy Family's flight to Egypt

929

lowly and riding upon an ass . . . and he shall speak peace" (9:9). People stripped palm fronds from the trees and waved them, crying: "Blessed is he who comes, the king, in the name of the Lord" (Luke 19:38).

Jesus went directly to the outer Court of the Gentiles of the Temple. There, merchants displayed their wares and money changers converted Roman denarii into obsolete shekels, the only currency acceptable to the priest. The next day a raging Jesus overturned the money changers' tables and drove out the vendors, invoking Isaiah 56:7: "Mine house shall be called a house of prayer," adding "You have made it a den of thieves" (Luke 19:46). Matthew relates that he also performed many healings. The Roman soldiers stationed at the Antonia fortress overlooking the courtyard did not intervene, perhaps because Jesus had the people on his side. He spent the night outside the city, but returned the following day to castigate the scribes and Pharisees. His sermons were received by an enthusiastic throng. They resented the heavy taxes imposed on them by both Roman and Temple authorities. The expulsion of the money changers was a direct challenge to the Temple council, or Sanhedrin, whose members included both Sadducees and Pharisees. With Passover imminent, tension was mounting. Attempting to get Jesus to make seditious statements against the Romans that would lead to his arrest, someone questioned him about taxes. "Render unto Caesar the things that are Caesar's and unto God the things that are God's," was his reply (Mark 12:17). The high priest Caiaphas, according to the Gospel of John, decided to take him prisoner and hand him over to the Romans, believing it better to sacrifice one man than the Jewish masses.

The Last Supper, painted by Giovanni Batista Tiepolo (1696–1770)

The Last Supper

Jesus ate the Passover meal that evening "in a large upper room" with his disciples, commenting that he would be betrayed by one who "dippeth with me in the dish" (Mark 14:13). During this meal, "Jesus took bread, and blessed, and brake it, and gave it to them, and said, 'Take, eat: this is my body.' And he took the cup, and . . . said . . . 'This is my blood' (Mark 14:22–24).

This last supper is symbolized in the Christian rite of Holy Communion. Celebrated in many denominations with many variations, it is also called the Eucharist (Lord's Supper). It involves the sharing of consecrated bread and wine (sometimes grape juice) in accordance with Jesus' command, "This do in remembrance

Painting by El Greco (1541–1616) showing Christ praying in the Garden of Gethsemane, while his apostles sleep and Judas is on his way with a band of Roman soldiers

930

of me." The Roman Catholic, Orthodox, Anglican, Lutheran, and several other Protestant denominations consider it a sacrament, something that is more than symbolic. They believe it to effect the actual communion of Jesus Christ with his faithful community. Other churches consider it an institution practiced in remembrance, not a sacrament. The Gospels do not get into theological debate on the extent to which Christ is present, but the subject became a matter of great debate in the Middle Ages.

Crucifixion

As Jesus predicted, he was seized later that night among the olive trees in the Garden of Gethsemane. His disciple Judas kissed him to identify him to the armed servants of the Sanhedrin. The remaining disciples fled. Interrogated by Caiaphas, "Art thou the Christ?" according to the Gospel of Mark, he answered, "I am." He was found guilty of blasphemy.

The following morning, a Friday now celebrated by Christians as Good Friday, they brought him before Pontius Pilate. Only the Roman procurator could pronounce the death penalty. Crucifixion, nailing the criminal to a cross, was the normal punishment for non-Roman criminals, rebel slaves, deserters, and insurgents. It was a gruesome death,

intended to take a long time. Pilate found him not guilty but the masses shouted, "Crucify him!" When Pilate offered to release him under the customary Passover amnesty, the mob asked him to free the condemned thief Barabbas instead. Pilate "washed his hands" of Jesus' blood and "delivered him to be crucified" (Matthew 27:24, 26). Jesus was taken to Golgotha ("place of the skull") on the hill called Calvary outside the city gate. He was nailed to a cross between two criminals. Before he died three hours later, he forgave the people condemning him. His body was taken down and buried before the Sabbath began at sunset, in accordance with Jewish law. The tomb was provided by Joseph of Arimathaea. Jesus' disciples scattered.

Resurrection

On the third day, a Sunday Christians celebrate as Easter, the tomb was found empty. Jesus was subsequently reported appearing to Peter, to James, to all the disciples, and to a gathering of some five hundred people. Word of this resurrection from the dead spread rapidly, reuniting the disillusioned followers. Belief in it is central to Christianity. It stimulated the formation of the first community of Jesus' followers in Jerusalem.

Miniature from the sixth century showing Christ on trial before Pontius Pilate

931

Marble relief from the cathedral in Split, Croatia. Before being crucified, Christ was flogged by Roman soldiers.

The Early Christian Church

The early Christian church was organized and administered by the disciples (or apostles, as Greek believers called them). They established a structure similar to that of the Jewish Essene sect, holding property in common. The members came together for a meal every Sunday, the day of Jesus' resurrection, to break bread and drink wine, as Jesus had done on the fatal Passover. The followers of the crucified Jesus still had a bad reputation. While eighty million inhabitants in the Roman Empire cared little, the disciples' free interpretation of the Torah made them atheists in the eyes of every pious Jew. The Sanhedrin created difficulties for them, soon turning to organized persecution. Even outside Jerusalem, Jew communities were harassed. Saul of Tarsus, a Jewish tent maker and son of a Roman citizen, was assigned by the high priest in Jerusalem to assist in this suppression. About 36 or 37 AD, on his way to Damascus, blinded by bright light, he

932

The first four books, or chapters, of the New Testament of the Bible are called the Gospels. They are attributed to the evangelists Matthew, Mark, Luke, and John, all of whom wrote in *koine*, the variant of Greek in common use. None of these men was concerned with biographical detail. Their focus was on the purpose and events of Jesus' life. They reported the master's sayings and stories of his miracles, death, and resurrection that were originally circulated only by word of mouth. Only Matthew and Luke narrate the story of his birth. Luke, a companion of Paul, wrote his version, probably from Corinth, about AD 80. Luke addressed a fairly sophisticated public that was originally pagan. He elaborated on the birth legends about Jesus with unmistakable parallels to non-Christian myths and stories, placing strong emphasis on his miracles. Tradition has it that he was a converted doctor who traveled with Paul and wrote not only the gospel attributed to him, but also an account of Paul's missionary travels, included in the New Testament as the Acts of the Apostles.

Matthew probably wrote his rendition about the same time, but addressed Jewish converts, emphasizing Jesus' Jewish lineage. Matthew was believed to be a farmer who left his home to follow Christ. After the crucifixion he preached throughout Palestine. Whether the gospel that has come down to us under his name was actually written by Matthew is difficult to know. This account stressed, above all else, that Jesus was really the Messiah promised in the Judaic scriptures. The work teems with quotations from the old prophets, yet at the same time offers detailed explanations of Jewish customs. It has been surmised that the author was writing for people who had some knowledge of the Jewish religion and would therefore be impressed by his references to the prophets, but that he himself was not a Jew.

Both he and Luke drew on the work of Mark, who probably heard the apostle Peter speak. The oldest gospel, that of Mark, emphasizes what Christ actually said. Modern theologians assume that his work is the closest to an original written source, now lost, which they designate by the letter Q (from *Quelle*, the German word for source). Addressed to the Christians of Rome in

Nero's reign, the Gospel of Mark was written about AD 70.

The last of the evangelists recognized by the church is John. John probably wrote around AD 100, using entirely different sources than the other three evangelists. It is hard to tell whether he was also the disciple John the Younger and/or the author of the Book of Revelations. He is primarily interested in the message of salvation, reflecting the mystical philosophy prevalent in his lifetime. Instead of tales of miracles, John concentrates on the profound dialogues between Jesus and his opponents. He looks beyond the historical details of the life of the man Jesus to their greater import, attempting to convey their theological significance. To him, Jesus did not simply die on the cross, but, "God so loved the world that He gave his only begotten Son, that whosoever should believe in him should not perish, but have ever lasting life" (John 3:16).

Mosaic from the mausoleum of Gallia Placida in Ravenna. It shows a bookshelf with the four gospels written by Mark, Luke, Matthew, and John.

933

heard Jesus ask, "Why persecutest thou me?" Suddenly converted, he changed his name to Paul and applied the same zeal once aimed at persecution to the dissemination of Jesus' teachings.

The movement, too, found a new name: Christians, after the Greek *Christos*, a translation of the Hebrew *Messiah*. This name reflected an increasing distance from Judaism. Pagans were admitted to this faith. Peter declared Jewish dietary laws invalid. Even circumcision was no longer practiced. This led to great conflict. Were the Christians a Jewish sect or not? Was the salvation Jesus offered intended only for the Chosen People of Yahweh, or for all humankind?

It was decided that salvation was open to everyone. Paul, in particular, defended this concept, carrying the new message to the world outside Palestine. He went to Asia Minor, Greece, and, finally, Rome, between 47 and 59, establishing new communities throughout the eastern Mediterranean basin. His letters to the churches became part of the New Testament, essential in defining the Christian faith.

Deacons (Greek for "servants") eventually took over much of the apostles' work, especially caring for the poor, acting as a lower order of clergy. The apostles continued as administrators, creating a hierarchy. Their successors, men of standing in Christian society, would be called bishops. Originally, there was no mention of celibacy. However, Paul was a confirmed celibate who advised against marriage. This led to the eventual prohibition of marriage for priests. It is said that women of the early church held power equal to males, a belief supported by the high esteem in which Jesus was known to hold women.

Detail from a painting by Andrea Mantegna (1431–1506) in which Roman soldiers are throwing dice for Christ's garments after he has been crucified

Miniature from a Greek manuscript from the eleventh century, depicting Christ appearing before his disciples after his death

The crucifixion of Christ, painted by Fernando Gallego (1440–c.1507)

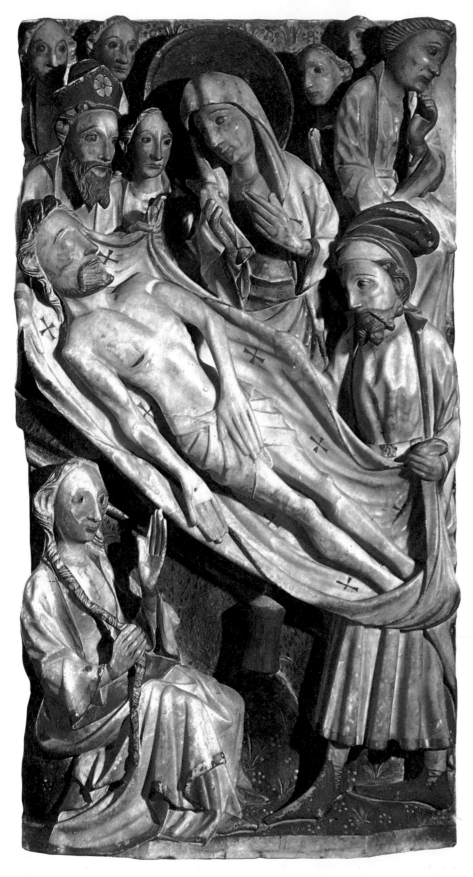

After his death,
Christ is taken from the cross
by his followers and his
mother Mary. Altarpiece from
the fifteenth century

Christians, in contrast, had no separate nation. Their refusal to have anything to do with the pagan rituals that were part of every aspect of Roman life caused them to be distrusted. Their talk of a Son of God, crucified but not dead, who would return to end the world or, at the least, overthrow Rome, made people fearful. Their encouragement of free thinking in the lower classes made them subversive in the eyes of authorities. Their Sunday meetings caused rumors of strange, possibly criminal, rituals. When they formed *collegia* (societies), the Christians violated Roman law. Such societies required official recognition or were considered conspiracies. Unrecognized collegia were regarded as conspiracies and the penalty for conspiracy was death.

When great sections of Rome burned down in AD 64, during the reign of Nero, much of the populace believed that the emperor himself had started it. To counter this rumor, Nero blamed the Christians. Their predictions that the end of the world (which would come with fire) was at hand sounded ominous. According to the contemporary Roman historian Tacitus, a great many Christians were arrested and sentenced to death "not so much on account of arson as because of their hatred of humankind." They were thrown to wild animals or nailed to crosses and burned. Among those killed were said to be the apostles Peter and Paul.

The official sponsorship of this first major persecution determined the attitude of the Roman ruling classes toward the new sect. Christians were widely regarded as subversives deserving the death penalty. Whether or not they actually committed any crimes was irrelevant. The name *Christian* was sufficient for conviction.

However, after Nero, large-scale persecution was a relatively rare event. In a letter he wrote to Pliny, the governor of Bithynia in Asia Minor, the Emperor Trajan decreed that Christians who renounced their faith and, as proof, performed sacrifices to the gods, could go free. Furthermore, the authorities were not to take the initiative in hunting out Christians. Only when one was formally accused by a private citizen would a trial be held. This would result in a verdict of not guilty and a penalty for the accuser if the accused Christian recanted. If more Romans had adhered to Trajan's rule, there would have been fewer Christians persecuted, despite the anxiety they aroused in the masses and the need of the governors to keep the population subdued.

A Subversive Society

Christianity grew, despite opposition from Jews and Romans alike. Like Jews, the Christians refused to worship any god but their own, but the Romans acknowledged this custom among the Jews and rarely compelled them to take part in pagan rites.

Fresco from the late second century in the catacombs of Priscilla in Rome. Depicted is the breaking of the bread in a communal Christian meal in imitation of the Last Supper.

Christianity Comes of Age

From Sect to State Religion

Christianity slowly expanded throughout the eastern Mediterranean basin from its original center in Jerusalem. The first disciples had carried it to Dimashq and Antioch by AD 38, to Asia Minor by AD 45, and to Rome by AD 49. The apostle Paul made four major trips aimed at spreading the Christian message between 47 and 59. By the time the Jewish Temple was destroyed in 70, Christianity was familiar to the Greek-speaking cities of the Eastern Roman Empire. Its membership spread from the Jewish community to Gentile people of many cultures, especially Greek.

By the second century, Christian communities known as *ecclesia* (assemblies) had been established in Greece. The Epistles to

Timothy and Titus (attributed to Paul but not necessarily written by him) reveal something of their organization. Their members were initially united only by their common faith, with no central authority either within the individual groups or over the church as a whole. Eventually, however, administration fell to one of the elders in each community. He came to be called the *episcopus* (supervisor), the Greek word from which "bishop" is derived. A hierarchy of priests and lower clergy, variously termed *deacons* or *presbyters*, formed under the bishops. At the weekly ceremonial meal, people read from a lively Christian literature. The letters of the apostle Paul, now codified as the Epistles of the New Testament, formed the basis of an

937

Christian sarcophagus dating from the fourth century. The central figure, with a lamb on its shoulders representing Christ as the Good Shepherd, was taken over from the Roman symbol of charity, the grape pickers from the Bacchic tradition.

emergent theology. Learned Christians began to hold discussions with pagan philosophers. They wrote *apologia* (apologies, or philosophic defenses), defending Christianity against pagan attacks. People began to formulate a distinct Christian ethic from the values implicit and explicit in the remembered words of Jesus. Elders established a liturgy.

By the third century, the bishop of Rome had great influence. He stood at the head of one of the greatest communities in the empire. The fact that the Roman Christians had been the first victims of persecution by the emperors gave them a certain prestige. Furthermore, Rome was the city of the apostle Peter, the man Jesus said would be the rock (*petra* in Greek) on which he would build his church. Regarded as Peter's heirs, the succeeding bishops of Rome gained importance but no real authority. At most, their influence was sufficient to enable them

to arbitrate communal disputes. The church was actually a federation of separate communities operating on an individual basis. They dealt with one another to the extent of giving support in time of need, exchanging literature, and providing lodging for members of other communities. When a universal rule was required, it was discussed until a consensus was reached. This very lack of a centralized structure appears to have been a great advantage in times of persecution, because the church could not be put out of commission simply by the seizing of a few leaders.

Suspicions

Officially, the Roman Christians operated outside the law, declared subversive elements by the authorities. They spoke of a kingdom of God; Roman officialdom thought this a temporal threat to the empire. However, the Christians were seldom actively hunted out. Emperor Trajan had actually forbidden that practice. Persecutions occurred primarily in the provincial cities in the excitement of a pagan festival, or in the wake of some catastrophe, when the Roman people wanted to see the Christians they called "atheists" punished for their "blasphemous" and "antisocial" lifestyle. In order to calm them down, the governors frequently gave in to their demands. There were also rumors that the Christians would murder children or indulge in sexual excesses at their secret gatherings. If charged, Christians could almost always escape death by renouncing their faith at the last moment. Many must have done so, but those who remained steadfast and died were honored as martyrs, "witnesses of Christ," by the remaining members of the community. It was believed that such martyrs went straight to heaven. Survivors prayed to them for support and intercession with Christ. There were occasions when Christians deliberately pro-

Picture of a miniature dating from the tenth century, representing John the Evangelist. According to Christian tradition he was the author of the Gospel according to St. John and the Book of Revelations. The latter was written on the island of Patmos, to which he was banished by the Romans.

A Christian raises his arms in prayer. This mural dates from the late second or third century and was discovered in the catacombs of Priscilla in Rome.

voked the authorities in order to die a martyr's death. They did this either from a kind of religious aspiration or to wash away their sins with their blood. The martyrdoms often made a great impression on the pagans. A faith that could inspire such deeds was not merely awe-inspiring, it was also attractive to many people.

The Church grew steadily. At the beginning of the third century the Christians formed one of the largest religious groups in the Roman Empire. Their solidarity, based on mutual support and general respect for specific leaders, was their strength. Persecutions were generally local and of brief duration. But as the century progressed, the empire entered a period of prolonged crisis. Foreign enemies invaded and plundered the provinces. Claimants fought for the imperial crown. Cities collapsed and wildfire inflation threatened to destroy the economy. Yet it was precisely in these disturbed times that the Church gained more adherents. The promise of a better life and an eternal reward for the righteous appealed to many.

As the Christian communities grew larger, new members could not always be easily absorbed. There was far less personal con-

The first Christians were often seen as members of a dangerous sect, and therefore persecuted. Miniature from a Greek manuscript dating from the eleventh century depicting a Christian being tortured

tact. The full community could no longer assemble in a single home. Special meeting places—Christian temples, so to speak—were built. The evening meals evolved into solemn celebrations. The communities obtained legal standing through a legal ruse: They presented themselves as burial societies that insured each member a decent funeral in return for a small contribution. Societies of this sort, usually organized by occupation, were a common phenomenon in the big cities. Outside of Rome the government had shafts dug in the ground where they placed the remains of the dead. Called catacombs, they were used for the dead of the common people from the *insulae* (the public apartment houses), and had walls covered with tablets of touching simplicity. The Christians built their own catacombs, which would shortly be used for quite different purposes.

In the middle of the third century, the emperor Decius decided to strengthen Roman society by renewing its ties to the old gods. He ordered all inhabitants of the empire to make sacrificial offerings to its traditional deities. Christians regarded it as idolatrous to comply, although many did. Many others were imprisoned for refusal. An unknown number remained faithful to their one God and were put to death for undermining the empire. The strongest Christian leaders were martyred. Eighteen months went by before a new bishop could be appointed in Rome. Meetings could be held only in secret. The Roman Christians descended into the catacombs at night and celebrated their ceremonial meals beneath the memorial tablets of the deceased. Decius's loyalty campaign, which seemed likely to exterminate the Christians, ended as suddenly as it began. The emperor was killed in the Balkans fighting the Goths, and his

Catacomb next to the Via Latina in Rome. Originally, catacombs were communal burial places for the Christians, who buried their dead in galleries carved in the soft tuffa stone. However, during the persecutions of the Christians the catacombs were also used as safe hiding places.

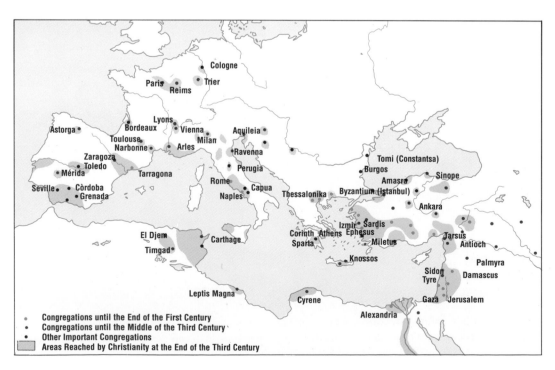

The Expansion of Christianity in the Roman Empire

- Congregations until the End of the First Century
- Congregations until the Middle of the Third Century
- Other Important Congregations
- Areas Reached by Christianity at the End of the Third Century

successor left the Christians in peace for the time being.

A severely battered Church could now begin to restore itself. Within a few years the communities had recovered. The cowards returned in ever greater numbers, creating a major problem in the Church, since the Christians who had remained steadfast were against readmitting them. By their weakness during the persecutions, people said, they had forfeited the right to salvation. However, little of this dispute was visible to outsiders. The Christians of the Roman metropolis contributed money to the smaller communities throughout the empire. Bishops gave large amounts to the poor.

At the same time, the imperial treasury was emptier than it had ever been. The Emperor Valerian had to defend a disintegrating empire against powerful foes. If he eliminated the Church, he would not only make its substantial possessions available for the border defense, he would achieve greater social unity in the empire. In 257 he issued an edict against the Church. This time, more than a loyalty oath or a sacrifice to the Roman gods was involved. Valerian wanted to destroy the entire ecclesiastical structure. He confiscated all its possessions, forbade Christian assemblies, and had the burial places seized. Shortly afterward he made the edict even more harsh, ordering the immediate execution of clerical officials. Any Christians in the ranks of the senators and nobles lost their property. Death awaited those who refused to renounce their god.

In 260, Valerian fell into the hands of his Persian archenemy Shapur I, and was killed. Valerian's son Gallienus succeeded him as Roman emperor and immediately stopped the persecution. He even issued an edict restoring the confiscated possessions. Once again the Church recovered with remarkable speed from the blows it had received. Once again, the problem of the repentant cowards reared its head. The gulf between those who were in favor of forgiveness and those who were against it became deeper. New converts came in streams. Even in the imperial army, many professed their belief in the Savior. High-ranking officers were baptized. The Christians were left untroubled by the government for about forty years. While the Roman Empire recovered from its setbacks, Christian bishops everywhere were able to expand their flocks. Impressive new buildings were constructed for religious services.

In the fourth century the Christians of Nicomedia had the Emperor Diocletian for their next-door neighbor, since their community center was built beside his palace. Diocletian ruled the empire from this city

Mural dating from the fourth century showing Adam and Eve covering themselves with fig leaves

Statue of the Good Shepherd dating from the sixth century

941

with an iron hand, reestablishing political order. He put an end to the turmoil caused by the soldier-emperors preceding him. The governors obeyed him, the army was disciplined, the taxes were paid. From Diocletian's standpoint, the Christians were traitors, a people disloyal to the empire. He had

Wall painting dating from the fourth century. It was discovered in the catacombs of Domitila in Rome and represents the Christian martyrs Veneranda and Petronella.

the army purged of them in 292. In 303 he extended his persecution to include ordinary citizens.

Diocletian went to work in the customary manner. First, he had the clergy exterminated. Then he granted mercy to those who made the requisite sacrificial offerings. Anyone who refused died a martyr's death. Mobs were incited to plunder Christian buildings before the authorities took care of the demolition. Diocletian's enormous power made his persecution particularly fierce. In Rome, the Christians were even obliged to close their catacombs.

However, Constantius Chlorus, the deputy

emperor in the West, did not proceed as seriously with his own efforts against the Christians. For both political and personal reasons, he took little action. In much of the rest of the empire, as well, Diocletian's campaign did not achieve its goals. Many of the emperor's subjects no longer supported it. By that time, perhaps 10 percent of the population was Christian. Many of the converts were sufficiently familiar to the majority or prominent enough to dispel rumors about them. Almost everywhere the persecution was sabotaged.

The End of the Persecutions

In 305, Diocletian surrendered his power. Galerius succeeded him in the eastern half of the empire, continuing the persecutions for a while. But his attention was soon diverted by the struggle that broke out in 306 among the various pretenders to the throne. Another factor in his ending of the persecutions was his realization that they were not eliminating Christianity. The religion had actually gained adherents in the face of official opposition. On his deathbed in 311, he issued an official edict of tolerance. For the first time, it was legally permissible to be a Christian in the Roman Empire.

Although his son and successor again adopted an anti-Christian policy, it was of short duration. Constantine had come to power. He may already have had secret Christian leanings for some time, but after his conquest of Rome in 312, he openly proclaimed his belief. A year later, in 313, he jointly issued the Edict of Milan with Licinius, the new ruler of the East. This restored the right to worship to the Christians. All property that had been confiscated was returned to the Church. The period from 311 to 313 marked a great turning point in imperial attitude toward Christianity. Rather than trying to abolish it, the emperor proclaimed it. A new era was beginning.

While Christianity gained more and more followers, some ancient cults underwent a kind of modernization. For example, the role of the Muses, formerly goddesses of arts and sciences, became much more important. They were believed to help humanity to reach immortality. Detail of a relief of the Sarcophagus of the Muses

The Fall of Paganism

Constantine and the Church

The Roman emperor Constantine was born in Nis (in modern Serbia) about AD 274 as Flavius Valerius Aurelius Constantinus, the son of Constantius I and Helena (later beatified). Made coemperor with his father in 305 and proclaimed emperor by his troops on the death of Constantius in 306, he had to fight to retain the throne. Just before the battle with his Italian archrival, Maxentius, in 312,

he dreamed that Christ told him to have *XP* (the first two Greek letters of the name *Christ*) inscribed on the shields of his soldiers. A believer, like his father, in the Roman sun god Sol, he attached great significance to the vision he had the next day, when he saw a cross and the Latin words *in hoc signo vinces* (in this sign you will conquer) superimposed on the sun. He attributed

Cameo depicting Constantine, his wife Fausta, and their three sons. The cameo decorates the cover of the *Codex Aureus* (*Golden Book*)

Shortly after 313 Constantine the Great initiated the construction of Christian basilicas. As the Christians themselves lacked any tradition of monumental architecture, the design of the basilicas depended heavily on classical Roman tradition. The drawing shows the Basilica Constantiana, better known as the Lateran Basilica, the first basilica built on Constantine's initiative. It was dedicated to the Redeemer. 1. Nave; 2. Aisles; 3. Fastigium; 4. Transept; 5. Apse.

his victory at the Milvian Bridge that day to Christ, and ended the persecution of the Christian minority when he became emperor. In 313, with his coemperor, Licinius, in the East, he issued the Edict of Milan, which legislated the toleration of Christians. Unwilling to take heavy-handed measures to outlaw paganism, given its majority position in society, he conducted a policy that consistently favored the Church, limiting paganism where possible.

The Church not only became a free institution, it now attracted both the poor and the ambitious. The emperor's example caused many to convert. That bishops everywhere could count on the emperor's support became evident when Constantine assumed sole rule of the Roman Empire in 324. He gave vast landholdings to the Christian communities, especially to the one in Rome. Within a few years the Church became the largest landowner in the empire, second only to the emperor. The authority of the bishop in each community was absolute, and the bishop of Rome rapidly gained moral and ecclesiastic authority over all other communities. The foundation for a hierarchical church was laid as the emperor moved toward making Christianity the state church.

In 325 Constantine convoked the first empire-wide meeting of church dignitaries in an effort to resolve discord about the mystery of the Trinity, with church dignitaries traveling at the empire's expense. At issue was the teaching of the Alexandrian priest Arius. He insisted, contrary to most Christians, that the Son of God could not also be God, that only God was the eternal creator, and that Jesus was created by him. The Alexandrian Athanasius argued that Christ had two natures, human and divine. Bishop Gregory of Nazianzus (called the

Theologian) and John Chrysostum of Antioch preached powerfully against Arianism. Constantine wanted unity. He would not allow his new source of power to weaken through internal feuding. He convened the council at the city of Nicaea in Asia Minor, with 318 bishops attending. Some of them agreed with Arius, while others vehemently condemned him. The council came to the decision that the Son of God was preexistent, and described him in the Nicene Creed as "God from God, Light from Light, true God from true God, begotten not made, of one being with the Father." It defined the Son as consubstantial with God, using the Greek word *homoousios* (of the same substance). It banned the teaching of Arius as heresy. Constantine exiled the priest and his major allies and declared the Nicene Creed state law.

Constantine adhered to these decisions but he was ambivalent. He did not want to antagonize the large group of Arian followers still influential in his court. In 334, influenced by the Greek church historian Eusebius of Caesarea, he recalled Arius from exile, banishing Athanasius instead, who would go in and out of exile five times over twenty years, and was eventually beatified for his adherence to orthodoxy. Emperor Constantius II advocated Arian doctrine, as did the bishop Eusebius of Nicomedia, the eventual patriarch of Constantinople. By 359 Arianism had been made the state religion, but two factions had evolved. Conservative semi-Arians agreed with the Nicaea decision but objected to the term *homoousios* as originating outside the scriptures. Neo-Arians preferred the use of *heteroousios* (different essence), implying that the Son was unlike

Marble statue representing Christ as a young man. It dates from c. AD 350. The statue's form is Hellenistic and is possibly one of the oldest statues of Christ known to us.

Cameo showing the portrait of Emperor Julian, who tried unsuccessfully to reestablish the cult of the traditional Roman gods

Remains of the Basilica of Constantine (or Maxentius) on the Forum Romanum in Rome. The building started during the reign of Emperor Maximianus (286–305) and the basilica was completed during the reign of Constantine.

the Father. Some of them, members of a group called the *Pneumatomachi* (warriors against the spirit), raised another argument. They insisted that the Holy Spirit was created, like the Son. The concept of the trinity, the doctrine that God exists as three Persons (the Father, the Son, and the Holy Spirit) united as one, is not explicit in the words of the New Testament. There, the word *God* usually refers to the Father. The phrase *Spirit of God*, used throughout the New Testament, usually refers to the presence of God rather than defining the nature of the Godhead. The Latin term *trinitas* (trinity)

was first used in the second century by Tertullian, a Roman theologian. Although it was part of the Arian controversy, the concept was not fully developed or addressed at the Council of Nicaea. That would occur in the fourth century, with the work of the theologian Augustine.

Constantius II died in 361. His successor, Valens, persecuted the semi-Arians. In 379, Emperor Theodosius recognized the Nicene Creed once more. It was reaffirmed at the second ecumenical council, held in 381 in Constantinople. At this point, the only ones still adhering to Arius's teachings were the

community gatherings were replaced by large ceremonies. Believers no longer shared an actual meal of communion, but attended a ceremonial mass in church. Bishops had become notable figures in the empire, princes of the church. They were given jurisdiction over territory rather than people, their sphere of influence defined by geography. The emperors promoted this hierarchy, since centralized authority made the church

Carved ivory dating from the fourth century. It was made in Alexandria, which was one of the most important cultural centers during the later period of the Roman Empire.

Germanic tribes on the fringes of the empire. Converted by Arian priests, they would hold their belief through the seventh century.

Patriarchs

Constantine, responsible for the reorganizing of the empire and making possible the rise of Christianity, was finally baptized on his deathbed. His successors, except for Julian, were all Christian. As the number of Christians increased over the fourth century, the problems of the third century resurfaced. The personal approach disappeared. Small

SORDI ELVENTIS ABLVIT AMBROSIVS AVRELII CAELESTIBVS

Detail of one of the porches of the cathedral in Milan, depicting an episode of the life of the city's famous bishop Ambrose

easier to control.

In the East, local communities were organized under the bishops (called *metropolites*) in each metropolis or provincial capital. Over the fourth century the bishops of Jerusalem, Antioch, and Alexandria became known as patriarchs. Each of these cities evolved as an autonomous center of Christianity. Once it was made his capital by Constantine, Constantinople developed rapidly, soon surpassing them. In 381 the emperor bestowed the title of patriarch on the bishop of Constantinople. His authority now rivaled that of Rome, enhancing the status of the emperor.

No one in the West was as influential as the bishop of Rome. The only patriarch in this area of the known world, he was called *Pappas* (Papa), the Greek form of address, or Pope. It became the official title for the head of the Roman Catholic Church.

In 395 the Emperor Theodosius divided the empire East and West. In less than eighty years, the pope, claiming Church supremacy over the state, acquired actual political power over the Western Roman Empire. In the East he was only nominally recognized. The Eastern Roman emperor ruled through his own instrument, the patriarch of Constantinople.

Paganism

Constantine had let the pagans worship as they pleased. His son Constans I, as the Western emperor, outlawed the worship of the Greco-Roman gods within the city limits but stipulated that the temples outside the cities must be respected. He probably did not wish to alienate the pagan rural populace. In any case, paganism did not disappear overnight. Smoke still rose from the offerings to the Olympian gods as it had for centuries. Many still adhered to the Eleusian Mysteries. In the Academy Plato had founded in Athens, philosophers debated the merits of Plato's ideals versus the new faith in Jesus Christ.

Constans I was assassinated in 350 by a usurper, Magnentius. His brother, Constantius II, made Eastern emperor on their father's death, defeated Magnentius in the Balkans, becoming ruler of the entire empire in 351. A strong advocate of Arian Christianity, he had no use for compromise with pagans. He summarily ordered the death penalty for anyone making sacrificial

948

The Christianization of Daily Life

In 313, Constantine the Great and Licinius, his coemperor in the East, issued the Edict of Milan proclaiming the legitimacy of Christianity. They ushered in a process that gradually made daily life in the Greco-Roman world more Christian. Imperial legislation under Constantine favored the Church but did not yet outlaw the traditional worship of the Greco-Roman gods. That would occur under his successors, all of whom were Christian except for Julian the Apostate. He attempted to reinstitute the earlier paganism of the empire. The other emperors established a series of laws to implement Christian ideas and values.

Constantine issued laws pertaining to the area of marriage and family as early as 313. Adultery by either husband or wife was made punishable by death. The sentence was to be carried out in a peculiar manner. The guilty party was tied up in a bag that also held a snake and a dog and thrown into the ocean. The extent to which this sentence was carried out is not known, but it presumably served as a deterrent. In 326, the rape of a virgin was declared a crime punishable by death. (This may have been intended to protect the growing number of celibate Christian women.) Laws protecting the family and children followed. The practice of abandoning infants, common in the ancient world, was made illegal in 315. Selling children into slavery was formally forbidden in 322. In 325, it was prohibited to separate slave families when sold. Divorce was permitted in limited cases in 331. Infanticide was forbidden outright in 374.

Pagan traditions such as organizing gladiator battles were made illegal in 325, although this decree was ignored for some time to come. Protected by the pagan majority in the Senate, the gladiator spectacle continued throughout the fourth century in Italy. One set of measures was aimed particularly at heathen practices. Those performing magic rituals were threatened with the death penalty in 318. A year later, the penalty was extended to people involved in private sacrifices made for the purpose of divining the will of the gods from the innards of the sacrificial animal. All pagan sacrifices were formally forbidden in 341, but the law was generally interpreted to mean only nocturnal and private sacrifices. Nocturnal sacrifices were barred again in 353. All pagan temples were ordered closed in 356, but the order was

widely disregarded. In 381 all animal sacrifices to the gods were banned once again and in 392 all pagan cults were formally outlawed by decree.

Over this time the Church received large donations of land and money while the bishops increased their judicial authority over nonecclesiastical matters. Their secular powers increased considerably in 316, 318, 321, and 333. The seven-day week that had emerged as standard in pagan times was Christianized on imperial orders. In 321 the first day of the week was declared a day of rest on the Sabbath model, chosen in remembrance of Christ's resurrection.

This enameled glass medallion shows a Christian woman of the Roman aristocracy, accompanied by two children. The medallion, from the fourth century AD, is set in a jeweled silver Byzantine processional cross from the seventh or eighth century.

Painting depicting a praying figure, flanked by two shepherds, from the *coemeterium* (catacombs) of Marius in Rome, from the third century

SYMMACHORVM

Detail of an ivory diptych made in memory of the wedding day of the daughter of the Roman senator Symmachus, who tried to convince several emperors to abandon Christianity and return to the traditional Roman religions

offerings, which were usually carried out under cover of night. Public offerings in daylight were still allowed. The court of Constantius II was a breeding ground for intrigue. He sent his cousin Julian to Gaul in 355 as commander of the Roman army, giving him the title *caesar*. Suspecting him of heresy, the emperor sent spies along, as well. A successful leader, Julian drove the invading Alemanni and the Franks back across the Rhine River. His soldiers proclaimed him emperor in 360. Civil war between the cousins was averted only by Constantius's death in 361.

Although reared a Christian, Julian equated the rampant corruption and intrigue in the empire with the Christianity of his uncle, Constantine. He took forceful measures to reform the administration and to restore worship of the Greco-Roman gods. Dubbed the "Apostate" for his heresy, he discriminated against Christians while supporting pagan cults wherever he could. He promoted officials who demonstrated the ability to be trained as *rhetors* (speakers) and forbade Christians to interpret classical texts in schools. He wrote vehement pamphlets and letters against Christianity and sided with theological rebels within the Church in order to foment discord. He organized a monotheistic mystical anti-Church, making sacrifices in his palace to the sun at dawn and sunset. In 363 he marched against the Persians in Mesopotamia. He was cut down by an arrow (which may not have been Persian) on June 26.

The army elected the Christian commander of the palace guard as his successor. He restored the moderate policies of Constantine: The heathens were left to themselves, while the Christians enjoyed his favor. This policy remained unchanged for the next twenty years. The emperors tolerated paganism, although conflicts arose at times.

In 367 Gratian became coemperor with his father, Valentinian I. After the old emperor's death in 375, he ruled jointly with his half brother Valentinian II until 383. Throughout his reign, he tried to eliminate all traces of paganism from the empire, beginning with his refusal of the traditional imperial title of *pontifex maximus* (chief priest). He abolished government financial support for pagan cults. He had an ancient statue of the goddess Victory removed from the Senate, the last bastion of pagan traditionalism. The majority of the senators came from anti-Christian clans loyal to the Greco-Roman gods and tried to maintain the traditions of ancient Rome during the sessions of the Senate. After the relocation of the imperial court to Constantinople, the Senate had been relegated to the status of a town council, losing most of its influence. The desperate senators sent emissaries to the emperor imploring him to return the statue to its proper place. The emperor did not even deign to receive the delegation. Gratian was killed by a usurper, Magnus Clemens Maximus, who was subsequently recognized by Theodosius as emperor of the West everywhere except Italy. Valentinian II continued to rule Italy. In 385, the senators tried again for an audience with the emperor. This time they got one. Valentinian II let them speak. Consul

Quintus Aurelius Symmachus presented a speech that was later published and widely distributed, but the mission was ultimately unsuccessful.

Symmachus was a noted orator and author. Through scrupulous attention to the details of traditional practices, he tried to revive the culture of Rome's Golden Age. His plea to Valentinian is a classic example of rhetoric. "Allow me to confess the reli-

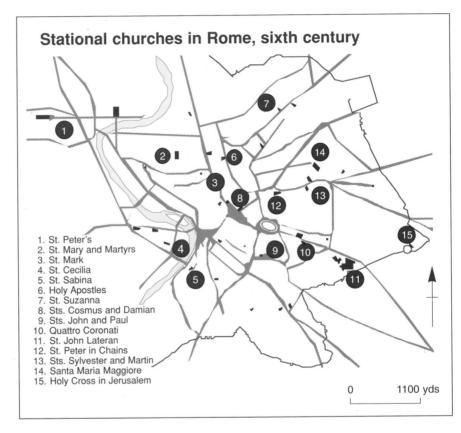

Stational churches in Rome, sixth century

1. St. Peter's
2. St. Mary and Martyrs
3. St. Mark
4. St. Cecilia
5. St. Sabina
6. Holy Apostles
7. St. Suzanna
8. Sts. Cosmus and Damian
9. Sts. John and Paul
10. Quattro Coronati
11. St. John Lateran
12. St. Peter in Chains
13. Sts. Sylvester and Martin
14. Santa Maria Maggiore
15. Holy Cross in Jerusalem

0   1100 yds

Most of the early Christians lived in the cities. The sixth-century map of Rome indicates numerous churches devoted to various saints. Some of them were so-called stational churches, a series of holy places that were visited by pilgrims.

Byzantine mosaic from Santa Maria in Trastevere. Trastevere is a district in Rome (on the far side of the Tiber) in which many of the early Christians lived.

Detail of a relief on the base of the obelisk of Theodosius. The emperor, standing amid his family and other spectators, is watching a race. In his hands he holds the wreath meant for the winner.

gion of my fathers," he exclaims, "and do not harbor a grudge against it. This religion subjected the universe to its laws. Its religion helped our ancestors to drive off Hannibal and to defend the Capitol against the barbarians." Symmachus adds that there should be no reason to reject the religion that made Rome great, and continues: "The god to whom we address our pleas is the same to all. The same heaven arches above our heads and we see the same stars and we are part of the same universe. The manner how one addresses one's Maker, is of little importance." Symmachus does not stop at defending his religion. He goes on to describe priests and priestesses who were robbed of their income by various improprieties. The oration created a great stir in intellectual circles.

The obelisk of Theodosius stands in Istanbul. Theodosius became emperor in 379 and succeeded in unifying the empire.

952

The great bishop of Milan, Ambrose, fiercely fought the elder Symmachus. "Everyone must serve the emperor," he argued at the court, "but the emperor must be humble before God. If you rule against God in this matter, the bishops will abandon you; you will enter the churches and not find a single priest to receive you." He addressed Symmachus, sweeping away his arguments with irony. "You say that the gods saved Rome from Hannibal and from the Gauls, but it was only the geese with their honking who roused the Capitoline guards from their sleep." (This refers to an incident of historical credibility.) "Why were the gods so slow to react during the Punic Wars? Had they decided to save Rome before the battle of Cannae, how many lives could have been spared?"

In 388 Maximus invaded Italy, where he was killed by Theodosius. Valentinian II was made emperor of the entire West. Ambrose's words had confirmed Valentinian in his views. He still refused to restore the statue of Victory to the Senate. His successor, who would receive two more delegations, likewise refused.

Theodosius, a Christian Emperor (347–395)

Theodosius had been selected to rule the East in 378 by Gratian, emperor of the West. An obsessed advocate of orthodox Christianity, he showed no tolerance toward paganism. He issued orders to destroy the altars and sanctuaries of the traditional gods throughout the empire. He appointed special commissions to see to the closing of the tem-

Picture of a Byzantine wall painting dating from the sixteenth century.
It represents the Council of Nicaea.

ples and the destruction of the cult objects. These measures against paganism often led to violent riots and mob lynchings. Bishop Martin of Tours (c.316–397), for instance, led a group of monks around Gaul felling the sacred oaks of the Celts.

The events in Alexandria were even more sensational. A mob stormed the Serapeum, an enormous temple that had been a place for the worship of the Egyptian god Serapis for centuries. Ptolemy I had established this cult as the official religion of his kingdom. Now Theodosius ordered the temple closed. The

The city wall of Istanbul (Constantinople). Emperor Theodosius commissioned the building of this wall in order to protect the city against invaders.

followers of Serapis locked themselves in the building and defended it as best they could. They finally surrendered, discouraged by the size of the mob and the imperial decree. A number of monks and converts stole into the holy chamber and began to hack everything to pieces. There was a great wooden statue of Serapis, clad with bronze plates, a scepter in his hand. A soldier climbed on the statue's shoulder and struck it in the face with an ax. When one of the bronze plates fell to the ground unhindered by divine wrath, other zealous Christians fell on the colossus and stripped off the bronze covering. Then they dragged the statue to the amphitheater and burned it.

Emperor Theodosius did not merely support Christianity, he sought to make it the only recognized religion in the realm. He stated that it was his will and wish that none of his subjects, in any village or city, would dare worship idols. He demanded that all inhabitants of the empire confess to the religion that "the Apostle Peter had taught the Romans and that the Pontiff Damasus and Bishop Peter of Alexandria are currently teaching." (This was the dogma of the Trinity as established by the Council of Nicaea.)

In 390 he had 7,000 people massacred in Thessalonica, Greece. He had charged them with revolting against him. Not all were guilty. Many innocent citizens were killed. The pope spoke out against the massacre and Bishop Ambrose of Milan excommunicated Theodosius, demanding public penance before he would lift the ban. The emperor dressed in a hairshirt and begged the bishop for forgiveness before the cathedral's altar. The people looked on approvingly. Theodosius was ordered to do penance for another eight months before he would be readmitted to the community of believers.

From the viewpoint of non-Christians, Theodosius had made a fool of himself. As they saw it, he had bowed to a few people, not before an almighty god rebuking him. The emperor could not allow such ideas to take hold. He and his officials continued their persecution with renewed vigor, attacking both Christian dissidents and heathens.

A change appeared imminent in 392 when Valentinian's own general, the Frank Arbogast, murdered him and appointed the Christian Eugenius as puppet emperor in his place. Arbogast demanded the people in the West recognize the new emperor. To win the support of the pagan senators, Eugenius allowed the statue of Victory to be placed back in the Senate at last. He placed all possessions that were confiscated from priests and temples at the senators' disposal, so as to render any subsequent seizure of them difficult. But the dream of pagan resurgence did not last. Two years later, Theodosius returned to Italy, vanquishing Arbogast and his pet emperor in September 394. He would rule both East and West only for the next four months, dying in Milan on January 17, 395. His young sons succeeded him, Arcadius in the East and Flavius Honorius, only twelve years old, in the West.

The official oppression that Theodosius had made an official state policy rapidly disappeared in high circles in Constantinople, but Christians still fought heathens elsewhere. In 415 the noted female philosopher Hypatia was slain in the street by a gang of fanatical monks in Alexandria. She concluded the long line of sages who had brought great acclaim to the School of Alexandria. In Athens, despite the oppression, Plato's Academy continued to exist. Throughout the fifth century philosophers taught Platonism tempered by mysticism, until the school was forced to close on order of Emperor Justinian in 529.

Christian Theology and Popular Belief

Creating a World Religion

Martyrs and Saints

About AD 36, Stephen, the first of the original seven deacons (lay clergy, below the apostles or priests) of the early church, was charged by the Jewish authorities with blasphemy. He had been preaching on the universality of Christ's message, the fall of the Temple, changes in the Torah (or Law), and the return from death (or second coming) of the crucified Jesus. He had irritated the Greek-speaking Jews in Jerusalem with his efforts at proselytizing. Brought before the Jewish council called the Sanhedrin, he was condemned to death by stoning. Saul of Tarsus (subsequently converted to become the apostle Paul) was there, and approved the decision (Acts 6, 7). Stephen, later canonized (declared a saint) is known as the Protomartyr, the first Christian martyr.

Stephen's death initiated both a cult of martyrs and an era of Christian persecution in Jerusalem. The small sect of Jesus' followers fled, carrying their new faith with them. In AD 64 Roman Emperor Nero blamed Christians for burning Rome and killed many of them, including, it is said,

Paul by the sword and Peter by upside-down crucifixion. Emperor Domitian, who took the throne in 81, tried to stop the wave of Christian churches across his empire by persecution. Thousands died on the cross, by the sword, by being burned alive, or in the lions' den for the amusement of the Romans. Martyrdom was believed to wash away the victim's sins, resulting in immediate sainthood. Christians saw heaven as populated with saints, each with a special day of remembrance. They were believed to give evidence of their power through a great variety of miracles.

Miniature from a fifteenth-century manuscript depicting the main Christian Church father Augustine (with a halo around his head as symbol of his holiness) and some of his students. Augustine lived from 354 to 430 and has greatly influenced the Western Christian Church.

Mary

Mary, the mother of Jesus, was referred to as the Mother of God by way of emphasizing the divinity of Christ. The scholar Irenaeus wrote: "The bonds in which Eve fettered us by her disobedience have been released by the obedience of Mary. What the virgin Eve bound by her fault has been freed by the Virgin Mary through her faith." In the fourth century the Greek title *Theotokos* (Mother of God) was disputed by the Syrian monk Nestorius. He claimed she should be called the Mother of Christ, not of God. In 431 the Council of Ephesus condemned Nestorius's view. Mary has been called Mother of God

Christian sarcophagus from the fifth century. It is decorated with scenes from the Old Testament.

since in both the Orthodox and the Roman Catholic churches.

Angels and Heaven

At about the same time as the veneration of Mary began, the veneration of the angels arose. The Jewish scriptures mentioned them as spirits or supernatural beings who served God. Paul discussed his reservations about the concept in his epistle to the Colossians. Only a century later, angels occupied a position of central importance. They were considered divided into seven groups and often individually named. The emperor Constantine built a church to the archangel Michael, who cast the evil angel Lucifer out of heaven. The fallen angel reigned over hell as Satan.

Christians believed in a heaven where the souls of the saved found eternal happiness among the angels and saints. They would live for eternity with the Lord. Heaven was assumed to be located on high. Hell, a place of fire and damnation, was thought to be at the center of the earth.

Baptism

All the concepts of the Christians reflected their desire to be assured of salvation. According to the evangelists, faith, hope, and love were not sufficient to achieve it. A baptism ritual was necessary. Ritual cleansing by water, especially that of the River Jordan, was provided for under Jewish law (Leviticus 11:25, 40, 15:5–7, Ezekial 36:25, and 2 Kings 5). It was also practiced in the mystery cults of Greece. The Christian custom of sprinkling with water to achieve remission of sins originated with the story of Jesus' baptism by John the Baptist (Mark 1:4, 9–11).

Adopting the Jewish notion that young children were part of the religious community, the early Christians probably baptized children as soon as they were born. The first-century Alexandrian theologian Origen (c.185–c.254) believed that infant baptism went back to the time of the apostles. Cyprian, in the third century, agreed with him. However, Emperor Constantine the Great, who was unwilling to receive the sacrament until he was on his deathbed, was not an exceptional case. Augustine is supposed to have regretted that he was baptized so late.

The Latin church father Tertullian (c.160–c.230) describes the ritual of baptism as it was performed in the Africa of his day. The candidates for baptism would begin with a formal declaration that they renounced the devil and his works. They went into a pool three times, taking a sip of milk and honey when they came out, to symbolize that they had been born again in Christ. After that, they were anointed with oil. The person performing the ceremony laid his hands on their heads to instill the Holy Spirit. Once baptized, they could participate in the Christian ceremonies.

The Eucharist

The central rite of Christianity is the communal remembrance of the Eucharist, or the Lord's Supper, the final meal Jesus took with his disciples the night before his crucifixion. It involves the sharing of consecrated bread and wine (which is what they ate and drank)

Limestone relief ❯ from the fifth century, carved with early Christian symbols

957

958

Early Coptic model for
making hosts, the sacred bread
that Christians eat during
Holy Mass

Angel painted
on a wooden panel,
made by Copts,
the early Christian
inhabitants
of Egypt and
Ethiopia

Flask, made by early Coptic Egyptians,
in which oil was kept that was used at sacred
rituals like anointments

Italian painting
from the fifteenth century
depicting St. Augustine
among his students

in accordance with Jesus' command, "This do in remembrance of me." The *Didache* laid down these rules: "Every Sunday, gather together to break bread and give thanks, after you have confessed your sins, so that your sacrifice is pure." Justin, who wrote an apologia for Christianity in the second century, described the ritual in considerably greater detail. The ceremony proceeded in the following sequence: 1) Bible reading; 2) sermon by the bishop; 3) prayer by all the congregation; 4) kiss of peace; 5) the deacons bring bread and wine; 6) prayer of thanks; 7) the sufferings of the Lord are recalled; 8) consecration, in which the bread and wine are believed to become the body and blood of Christ; 9) intercession for the people; 10) prayer of thanks by the congregation; 11) holy communion; 12) collection for the poor.

Christian churches disagree today, as they have for centuries, as to whether this rite is a sacrament, something more than symbolic, or an institution practiced in remembrance. In any case, by the fourth century the liturgy had four major variants, named after Antioch, Alexandria, Rome, and Gaul.

Forgiveness

In spite of their attempts at pious practice,

regardless of their faith and participation in church ritual, people sinned. The church debated what to do with repentant sinners. Jesus had bidden the apostles to forgive people their sins, but there was controversy over how far this was to be taken. Tertullian, for example, was extremely severe. Writing about 200, he contended that forgiveness could only be obtained by baptism, as "the second protection against hell, but the last." He regarded sins committed after baptism as unforgivable. In 220, Pope Callixtus expressed himself much more mildly. Sins were to be forgiven as often as necessary,

In the foreground of this photograph the ruins of Hippo (Anaba in North Africa) can be seen, the city where Augustine was bishop. In the background is the basilica that was built in his memory.

as long as the sinner was repentant and determined not to sin again. Repentance had to be expressed openly and the sinners had to do penance for their misdeeds. In general, this meant an exclusion from the community of the faithful for some period of time. In serious cases, the excommunication lasted for an entire lifetime. However, even in this case the possibility of forgiveness was not denied. The sinner could repent on his deathbed, receiving the last rites of forgiveness.

Augustine

Study of the holy scriptures kept pace with theological debate. By the second century, Christian thinkers argued with pagan philosophers everywhere. The Roman Catholic

The Confessions of St. Augustine

About 400, Augustine wrote his autobiographical book, *Confessiones* (*Confessions*). It is one of the few personal writings in the literature of antiquity. Only the letters of Cicero and Julian the Apostate reveal as much of the character and personality of the author. In this work he detailed the process of his conversion and his life before it. With great frankness he set forth his own desires and weaknesses. He had lived for fifteen years with a Carthaginian woman whose name he does not reveal, who bore him a son in 372. Greatly interested in the study of various philosophies, he was long attracted by Christianity, but wrote that he prayed, "Give me chastity and continence, but not just now."

Augustine described his inner conflict: "I suffered and tormented myself and turned about in the chains that still held me with a weak shackle, which nevertheless kept me in bondage. I said to myself: Onward! Delay no longer! I resolved to begin and did nothing. I fell back into the abyss of my former life. And when that elusive moment drew nearer, in which my being was to be transformed, I became more and more anxious and troubled. And the smallest trifles, the most idle trivia, my old friends, plucked me by the clothes of my body and murmured: Are you going to part from us? What? Shall we never keep each other company again? They no longer attacked me directly, as they once did, petulantly and boldly, but with a timid whisper in my ear. . . . This internal struggle was a duel with myself. I ran back into the garden and gave free rein to my tears, crying out: How long, oh Lord? How long? Tomorrow? Tomorrow? Why not now? I spoke and wept with all the bitterness of a broken heart. And suddenly, I heard from an adjacent house a child's voice, or the voice of a young girl, that was singing and repeating these words: Take and read, take and read. It occurred to me that the words could be the refrain in a child's game, though I could not remember anything of the sort. I went back to the place where I had been sitting earlier and where I had left the book with the epistles of Paul. I picked it up and opened it, and my eyes fell upon the following words: You shall not live in excess and debauchery, but follow Jesus

Christ. I had no need to read further. I had scarcely finished reading the line, when something like a light spread through my heart and dispelled the darkness of my uncertainty. I was about to meet my mother. I told her all that had happened, and she rejoiced when she heard my story. '

Like the apostle Paul before him, Augustine emphasized the weakness of the human will. He saw his conversion as something he was incapable of on his own. He defined it as a matter of grace, the result of God's mercy.

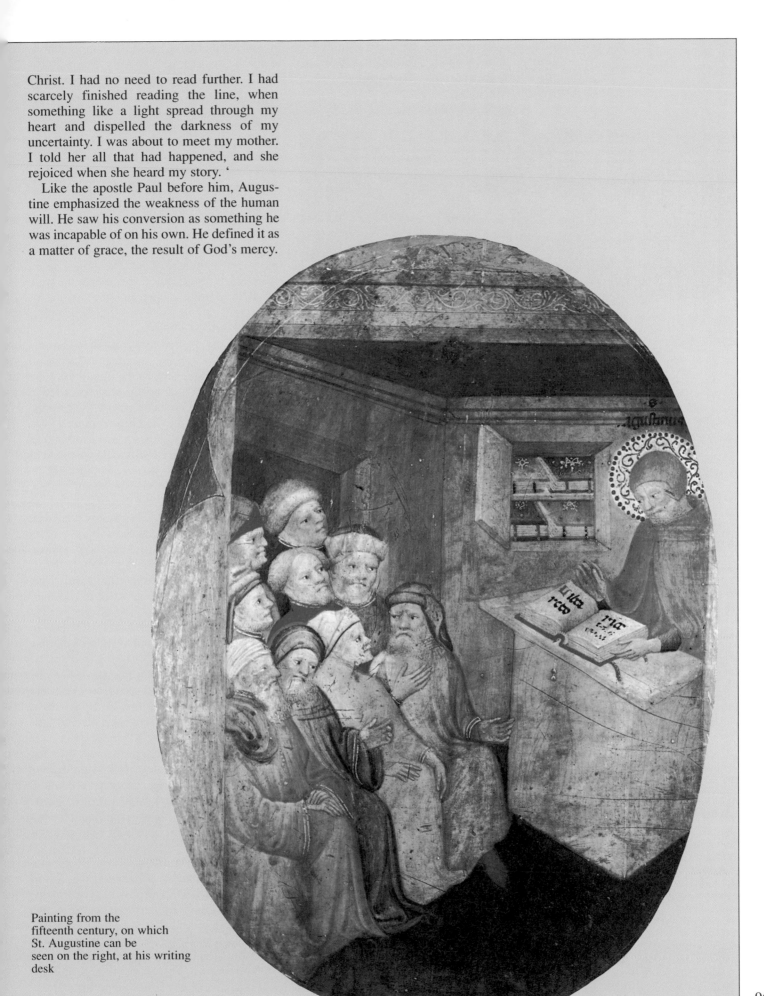

Painting from the fifteenth century, on which St. Augustine can be seen on the right, at his writing desk

Church still venerates the early church fathers, scholars who molded Christian thought into what, to a large extent, it continues to be today.

The greatest of them was Augustine. His

De civitate Dei (The City of God) is Augustine's most well known book. This medieval miniature depicts the two cities described in this book: the city of God *(above)* and the city of the earthly world *(below)*.

many works reveal great wisdom and literary skill. Augustine was, in fact, a brilliant writer who can take his place among the great authors of world literature. He was born in 354 in the small town of Tagaste, Numidia (now Souk-Ahras, Algeria). His father, Patricius (who died about 371), was a short-tempered pagan who eventually converted to Christianity. He took little interest in his son. Such upbringing as Augustine received was provided by his devoutly Christian mother, Monica. She was subsequently canonized by the Roman Catholic Church. Augustine's family scraped the money together to send him to study with the rhetoricians of the African metropolis Carthage. He lived for fifteen years with a Carthaginian woman of unknown name who bore him a son in 372. He named the boy Adeodatus, Latin for "gift from God."

His reading of *Hortensius*, the lost work of the Roman Marcus Tullius Cicero, inspired Augustine to seek truth, as it advocated. This essay argues that people must lead a moral life if they wish to be happy. In 373, he adopted Manichaeism, a popular Persian philosophy. Nine years later he gave it up for Skepticism, the Greek doctrine that the truth of all knowledge is open to question.

Conversion

In 383, accompanied by his mother, his mistress, and his child, Augustine sailed to Rome. There he came to the attention of the pagan senator Symmachus, who had tried to convince the Christian emperor to restore the statue of Victory that had been removed from the Senate. Symmachus set Augustine up as a teacher of rhetoric in Milan. Augustine sent his mistress back to Africa so he could be free to arrange a marriage in higher circles. Although influenced by Neoplatonism, he remained interested in Christianity. One day, he wrote, he heard a voice telling him to "Take up and read," which he took to mean the Scriptures. Opening to Romans 13:13–14, he read, "Put on the Lord Jesus Christ and make no provision for the flesh, to gratify its desires." He was converted. He and his son were baptized on Easter Eve in 387 by Italy's paramount bishop, Ambrose of Milan.

Augustine returned to Tagaste, where he attempted to establish a monastery with his philosophical study group. He spent three years writing essays about such diverse subjects as music and heresy. Ordained in 391, he was invited to Hippo (now Annaba, Algeria) as an assistant priest. Although he continued his writing, he also became a prominent local orator. When the old cleric died in 395, Augustine was appointed bishop of Hippo, a position he would hold until he died in 430.

The little diocese of Hippo ran of its own accord and, unlike his colleagues, the bishop had no ambitious plans for advancement. Completely engulfed in his intellectual activities, he was not interested in long journeys, intrigues, or visits to the court. In the peace of his small cloister, he dictated his thoughts at great speed to a stenographer, sending a flow of publications from Hippo throughout the known world. There was good cause for powerful polemics. The Church was divided with heresy even as the empire was assaulted by barbarians. (Rome itself was vandalized in 410.) Augustine was well prepared for this heated intellectual climate. He sent forth fierce attacks on heresy until the end of his life, defining the freedom of human beings and their role in achieving salvation or damnation. His first broadsides were aimed at the Manichaeans, his former companions.

Manichaeism

Manichaeism was named for its third-century founder, the Persian Mani, who saw himself as the final prophet in a line that included Zoroaster, Buddha, and Jesus. That alone put his philosophy in conflict with the Christian Augustine. He objected, as well, to its picture of a world forever in conflict between good and evil, since Augustine saw the world as created by God and therefore good. Believing in the uniqueness of the soul, he further rejected the Manichaean concept of the transmigration of souls. (The celibate and vegetarian Manichaean "elect" could attain the kingdom of Light after

Page from a medieval manuscript of the sermons of St. Augustine

Byzantine panel dating from the sixteenth century, with a painting of St. Anthony

963

death. The lower "auditors," people who served the elect, could only hope for rebirth as members of the elect.) Augustine, in contradistinction to Mani, insisted on the role of both free will and divine grace in salvation.

Predestination

Augustine's contemporary, the British monk Pelagius, denied the concept of original sin. He published a number of works so controversial that the African bishops held a synod to discuss them. In Carthage he was accused of promulgating nine errors, namely: 1) that Adam, created mortal, died for that reason, not because of his inherent sin; 2) that he alone was punished for his sin, rather than all humankind; 3) that people, like Adam, were born without sin; 4) that just as Adam's sin had not brought death to humankind, so Christ's resurrection had not brought the prospect of their own; 5) that if unbaptized children died, they would go to heaven; 6) that even before Christ, people died without sin; 7) that the Law of Moses was as important for salvation as the New Testament; 8) that people can live without sin, as a matter

Relief on the bronze door of the sacristy in Florence depicting Ambrosius (c.334–397), bishop of Milan and one of the four church fathers of the Christian Church. He is the one in the middle.

Part of a Spanish altar from the thirteenth century, on which the archangel Michael and Satan are shown weighing a soul

of their own choice; 9) that the wealthy, even if baptized, must abandon their possessions to achieve salvation.

The bishops condemned Pelagius, with the support of the pope in Rome. Pelagius, meanwhile, placed himself under the protection of the bishop of Jerusalem. From Palestine he continued to propagate his views, which appalled Augustine. In his efforts to counter them, he defined his own doctrines of divine sovereignty, original sin, grace, and predestination.

Augustine was more concerned with the problem of original sin than with the origin of souls. Since the Scriptures offered little help on the questions of when souls were created and how they were connected to the body, he concluded: "This means that it is unnecessary to solve the problem, because otherwise the Scriptures would have been more explicit." Origen believed that souls

L'inferno, one of the mosaics in the Baptistery in Florence. The man in Satan's mouth is Judas.

965

wait for their birth from the beginning of time. Others believed that they were created by God at the moment of conception or at the moment of birth. Augustine had little interest in these questions. The crux of the matter, as he saw it, was whether or not all souls had become sinful through Adam's fall. Based on the Scriptures, Augustine answered the

Miniature that illustrates a fifteenth-century manuscript of *De civitate Dei*

first question with a resounding yes. The soul could be cleansed of sin, but only by the grace of God. This was precisely the opposite of the conclusion Pelagius had reached. According to him, God had given people reason and freedom so that they could decide for themselves whether to be saved or damned. Salvation depended on the will of each individual to live without sin.

Augustine's answer was the concept of predestination. Even before birth, he said, people were predestined to go to heaven or to hell. He pointed to his own experience, which had shown him how fruitless it was to make personal efforts to be saved. What had the advice of his mother or reading or sermons really done for him? In a single moment, he felt, God accomplished what all

these could not in Augustine's twenty years of spiritual wrestling. Augustine could not believe that human beings were created without pattern to their lives. God, he insisted, must know what their lives would hold in store for them. Yet how God's plan and God's mercy interact with human freedom of will, he said, remain a mystery beyond the grasp of human understanding. The dilemma still exists. Augustine's theology can be interpreted to mean complete predestination. The question is the extent to which people earn salvation or damnation through the exercise of their own will.

Works

In about 400 Augustine wrote the autobiographical work *Confessiones* (*Confessions*) on his early life and reasons for adopting Christianity. Between 413 and 426 he wrote twenty-two books that make up *De civitate Dei* (*The City of God*), an apologia for Christianity. Pagans were inclined to hold the new religion responsible for the demise of the Roman Empire. This idea was especially popular after Alaric sacked Rome in 410. To refute it, Augustine raged against pantheism in ten books, then traced the history and development of the Christian church in another twelve volumes. In these, he explained why he felt Christianity should succeed paganism. It is a Christian view of the great struggle between good and evil. History, he wrote, is moving slowly toward the climax of the Last Judgment, when the citizens of the City of God would be saved and the rest damned.

Augustine wrote hundreds of letters, 270 of which are collected in the *Epistles*, written between 386 and 429. He wrote *Homilies* about books in the Bible and treatises: *On Free Will* (388–395), *On Christian Doctrine* (397), *On the Trinity* (400–416), and *On Nature and Grace* (415). In *On Baptism: Against the Donatists* (400), he took on yet another major heresy of his time. The Donatists contended that the Christian sacraments had to be administered by priests who were sinless. Since he believed no human was born in that condition, he argued the point. One of his last works was *Retractions*, a revision of much of his earlier writing.

Augustine died in Hippo on August 28, 430, with the Vandals at the gates. They brought a new power structure and a new society, but Augustine's work was not lost. His theology was the basis for the theories that Christian scholars would construct for centuries.

Miniature from an eighth-century manuscript depicting Benedict giving his monastic rule to the monks of Monte Cassino. This so-called *Regula Benedicti* was the most widely used monastic rule in the Middle Ages—during the reign of Charlemagne (c.800) it was even made compulsory for all monasteries of his realm.

Monasticism

Seclusion in the Name of God

Paul of Thebes

The history of Christian monasticism traditionally begins around 250 with the legend of a wealthy Christian named Paul (not to be confused with the apostle Paul). He fled to the desert to escape the persecutions of the Roman emperor Decius. After the death of his persecutor, he chose to remain in the desert, living a life of hardship in an effort to overcome evil. Legend would have it that he continued to deprive himself of human companionship, mortifying himself for nearly a

Basil, his brother Gregory of Nyssa, and Gregory of Nazianus on a miniature from the ninth century. Each of them holds a book in his hand as a sign of their great knowledge.

century. He was canonized (declared a saint) by the Roman Catholic Church. In 340 Anthony of Egypt sought him out. It is said that the two hermits had such a lengthy conversation that God sent a raven to bring them bread for a meal.

St. Anthony (c.251–c.350)

Anthony himself is often cited as the first Christian hermit. Following Paul's example, he withdrew from the world and went to the hills above the Nile River. The first hagiography (biography of a saint) was written about him by Athanasius. In it, Anthony exhibited great interest in the world he had renounced. Writing in Coptic, he asked: "What are the people up to? Do cities still exist? Who rules the earth? Do people still fall prey to the devil?"

Anthony lived a life of deliberate hard-

ship, first in an unused rock tomb and then, for twenty years, in the ruins of an Egyptian fortress. He found even this too luxurious, leaving it to travel the barren windy desert between the Nile and the Red Sea. He was prey to temptation everywhere, the story says. Satan beleaguered him with an army of demons, but the saint emerged victorious. One of the earliest Christian ascetics, Anthony searched for solitude and was repeatedly interrupted by people following him. Many were fleeing the persecutions of the Roman Empire for the wilderness. About 311, Anthony helped Christians in Alexandria who were persecuted by the emperor Maximin. He created a loose community of hermits who sought personal solitude within a common monastic life, called *koinos bios* in Greek. From this comes the word *cenobite*, used to describe the kind of eremitic (hermitlike) lifestyle Anthony established first in Alexandria and then in the desert. Rules for his groups were later drawn up by his friend and biographer, Athanasius.

Motives for the ascetic life were legion and complex, sometimes social rather than religious. In Egypt and the regions of Syria and Palestine, some Christians became ascetics, motivated by their yearning for closeness with God. As society slowly became more Christianized, pagan idols and temples began to disappear. To many Christians, the gods were demons who had retired to the desert when their dwelling places among people were destroyed. To fight them, or the devil himself, a pious Christian could seek them out in the wilderness. A strong movement toward lives of piety began at the end of the third century, giving new forms to the worship of Christ. Some chose solitude, living as pious hermits. Others sought the ideal of a community of the holy, especially in the East.

Monasticism in the East
St. Pachomius (c.320)

Pachomius, an Egyptian soldier who became a desert disciple of Anthony, founded what is considered the first monastery on an island in the Nile River. Pachomius (later canonized by the Roman Catholic church) established a set of cenobitic monastic rules, the first of their kind. He put the monks under the authority of a superior, called an abbot or

Relief from the sixth century depicting Pachomius. He was one of the desert fathers who lived in Egypt in the fourth century.

an archimandrite, who ensured that they abided by the rules. The central idea was to give each individual monk as much opportunity as possible for his own purification. The concept of service to others, a guideline in so many subsequent monasteries, was largely absent. Aspiring monks were required to wait seven days in front of the monastery's gate before being admitted. Once accepted, they were subjected to a novitiate, or trial period, lasting three years. Finally admitted to the community, they lived lives of detach-

A group of Christians flees the Arians.
Miniature from the ninth century

Detail of a painting
by Starnina, representing
some monks and the church
of their monastery

St. Anthony
(c.251–c.350)

Much is known about St. Anthony, the canonized hermit, from an extensive description
Bishop Athanasius of Alexandria wrote in the
middle of the fourth century. It was the first
hagiography (biography of a saint), a literary
genre that was to become very popular with
Christians in the Middle Ages.

Athanasius sketches Anthony's character,
then the tale of his conversion. At age twenty,
the wealthy Anthony is so impressed by the
Bible teaching of "Go, sell what you possess
and give to the poor, and you will have trea-
sure in heaven" (Matthew 19:21) that he dis-
perses his inheritance and goes to live as an
ascetic. He becomes a pupil of the ascetics in
his village, outdoing them in his dedication.
When temptations come from Satan, Anthony
is able to resist them. He leaves the village
and moves into an empty tomb. The devil
tries in vain to enchant him with obscene
images, evoking even greater purity on the
hermit, who justifies his way of life: "Like the
fish which dies out of the water, the hermit
dies out of the desert."

Anthony moves deeper into the desert to
face the devil. People visit him from the civi-
lized world seeking advice, or abandon their
homes to join him. Anthony, obeying a divine
voice, moves alone ever deeper into the
desert. Again, demons appear to tempt him in
various ways. He has a vision and a series of
revelations. People descend on him again
from all directions. He organizes them into a
loose community. In the final section, God
notifies Anthony of the time of his death. The
saint prepares himself and leaves instructions
with his students for his burial.

The almost complete lack of hard facts and
chronological data of this hagiography
became characteristic of the genre, as did
tales of the saint's visions and mysterious
knowledge. Anthony sees the motives of the
people who come to him. He reads their

ment from the material world. They took
vows binding them to the rules, including
celibacy. (Some early churches in Syria
required all their baptized members to live a
life of celibacy. As the Church gradually
grew into a mass movement, this rule could
not be enforced in the larger community, but
it was a common monastic requirement.)

The monks secured a livelihood from agriculture, raising livestock and weaving mats
and baskets. The head of the community

organized the division of labor. The monks
lived in groups of three in cells. They ate
meals communally with their heads covered,
forbidden to talk. Permanent silence was
required. Only in rigidly circumscribed

thoughts and foresees the moment of his death. All this is written to prove that he is a saint. The same purpose is served by the witnesses who are quoted to testify to the predictions and miracles. Anthony is described as attaining increasingly saintly qualities, to the point where he can finally vanquish Satan. Later hagiographies follow this pattern. The saint becomes a man of God, dissociating completely from normal mortal life to gain heavenly status. A type of modesty distin-

guishes the Christian saint from many a pagan miracle worker who would boast that his miracles arise from his own supernatural power. The Christian saint claims to perform miracles or utters prophecies only by means of his bond with God: It is not he, but God who works these miracles through him. Anthony warned, 'Do not rejoice when the spirits obey you, but that your name shall be written in heaven."

The life of St. Anthony has been a source of inspiration for many people and also for Salvador Dali. In this painting from 1946, Anthony fights against luxury, comfort, and passion.

instances were the monks even allowed to express themselves through gestures. Despite the extreme strictness of his rules, Pachomius attracted thousands of followers. He founded nine other communities on the

same model before he died. One of them, supervised by his own sister, was established for women. A hundred years later, an estimated 50,000 monks lived in Pachomian monasteries.

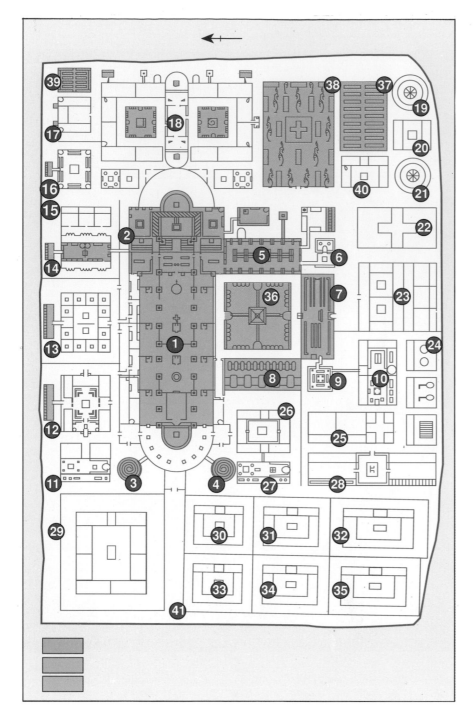

The so-called cross of Desiderius that was made in the seventh century. Halfway down the foot is a medallion with a portrait of a Roman noble lady and her son and daughter, which is shown in close-up on page 949.

St. Basil of Caesarea (c.329–379)

Yet it was not Pachomius but Basil of Caesarea who is known as the patriarch of eastern monasticism. He was born in 329 in Caesarea Mazaca (modern Kayseri, Turkey) near the Black Sea. A member of a wealthy family, he journeyed to Athens and then Constantinople to train as an orator. One of his classmates in Greece is said to have been the future Roman emperor called Julian the Apostate. Following his studies, Basil undertook a long journey through Palestine and Egypt. There he saw the desert monks, the subject of much academic discussion. Basil showed great interest in their road to salvation, adopting it himself beside the Iris River in Neo-Caesarea. He made an extensive study of the various forms of monasticism, dividing them into four categories. These were the hermits, eremitic desert dwellers; the ascetics, who lived together in unorganized communities; wandering holy men; and monks living in organized monasteries. Basil opted for monasticism, considering a community of spiritually oriented people ideal only if it were regulated toward the ideal of brotherly love. "The solitary life has only one goal, the service of its own interests. That is clearly opposed to the law of love."

Basil was not able to enjoy his isolated paradise for long. The Church called on him to perform important assignments in the world outside it. Before he left the river, however, he drew up most of a monastic rule still used by some Roman Catholic orders and most Orthodox monasteries in the East. Twenty of them circle Mount Athos in modern Greece. Basil's long rules include fifty-three questions and answers. His short rules provide solution to 303 problems that might arise in a monk's life. He believed that asceticism approached pure Christianity and that monks were the true believers, obliged to imitate Jesus and the apostles to the tiniest detail. To uncover those details, he said, monks must study the scriptures. The most talented among them would be given opportunities to do so by the abbot. These scholarly monks also represented a board of advisors to the abbot, accorded the authority to act as a complaint board for individual monks on their treatment. When the abbot was not available, a learned monk would

The famous plan of the monastery of Sankt Gallen (c. 820)
1. church; 2. scriptorium with a library on the first floor; 3. St. Michael's tower; 4. St. Gabriel's tower; 5. bedroom for the monks with a heating room downstairs; 6. bathroom for the monks; 7. dining room for the monks; 8. wine and beer cellar for the monks with a provision room downstairs; 9. kitchen for the monks; 10. bakery and brewery for the monks; 11. kitchen, bakery, and brewery for important guests; 12. residence for important guests; 13. school for nonresidents; 14. house of the abbot; 15. kitchen, cellar, and bathroom for the abbot; 16. room for bleeding; 17. doctor's room; 18. residence for novices and hospital; 19. goose pen; 20. chicken pen where the goose keeper lived as well; 21. chicken pen; 22. granary; 23. rooms for workmen; 24. mill; 25. building for coopers, cart makers, and granary for the brewers; 26. guest house for pilgrims and the poor; 27. kitchen, bakery, and brewery for pilgrims and the poor; 28. stable and ox stable with room for the caretaker; 29. residence for the following of the emperor; 30. sheep pen with a room for the shepherd; 31. goat pen with a room for the herd; 32. cow barn with a room for the keeper; 33. residence for servants and the royal followers; 34. pigsty with a room for the keeper; 35. stable for horses and fowl with a room for the keeper; 36. garden; 37. kitchen garden; 38. cemetery and orchard; 39. herb garden; 40. gardener's house; 41. entrance road

973

take his place.

Obedience to the abbot was mandatory. Rebellion was treated as a disease. The rebel would be sent to the hospital ward. If he did not improve, he was exiled from the community because "insubordination and distrust are the result of a number of sins, doubtful

A portrait of
St. Anthony on a Byzantine panel from the sixth century

faith, pride, and misbehavior." Eight times a day the monks were required to meet in prayer. Basil described these meetings in mystical and poetic terms. Prayer did not release the monks from labor. "He who wants to eat must work," he insisted, in a monastic rule that draws on Paul the Apostle. Basil did not require absolute poverty of his monks. They were permitted personal possessions and allowed to live in solitary rather than shared cells inside the monastery. To Basil's way of thinking, this was logical, since his goal was not to establish a model community, but to allow each individual to develop his greatest spiritual potential. In practice, however, this freedom fostered abuse.

About 360, Basil founded an order of monks (the Basilian). The young scholar had no difficulty setting up his own monastic experiment; his personal estate was adequate for the purpose. In 370, after long service to the bishop of Caesarea, he was elected to that position himself. He held the post until he died on January 1, 379.

In addition to his famous law, Basil wrote three books opposing the Arian theologian Eunomius, collectively titled *Against Eunomius*. Other works include a treatise *On the Holy Spirit and Moralia*, a collection of verses from the New Testament.

Three generations of Basil's family are venerated as saints, including his grandmother Macrina; his parents, Basil and Emmelia; his sister Macrina; and his brothers Peter of Sebaste and Gregory of Nyssa. Basil, Gregory, and their friend St. Gregory of Nazianzus are called the Cappadocian Fathers.

Stylites

Some of the early Christians undertook various forms of self-mortification in their efforts at piety. They sought the salvation once believed to have been achieved only by martyrdom. In the fifth century St. Simeon Stylites, a Syrian monk, first buried himself up to the chin for months on end. Later he bound his waist until the skin rotted. Finally, he literally stood atop a sixty-foot-high pillar for thirty-seven years, preaching twice a day. A railing set in the top of the column kept him from lying down and he refused to sit. His food was brought up by ladder. Individual ascetics imitated him for seven centuries on their own pillars.

Monasticism in the West
St. Athanasius (c.293–373)
Athanasius was born in Alexandria and given a classical education prior to his theological studies. Rising through the church ranks, he was made bishop of Alexandria around 328 and posthumously canonized. Most famous for his opposition to his fellow Alexandrian priest Arius, he insisted that Jesus, the Son of God, was of the same essence as God the Father. (He used the phrase *homoousian in nature* from the Greek *homoous* for "substance".) The Council of Nicaea in 325 agreed, declaring Arianism heresy. (Arius contended that the Son was

created by and of a different substance than God.) As the two priests fought for imperial approval from Constantine I, Athanasius was banished five times. However, he had time to introduce the cenobitic form of monasticism to Rome and northern Italy. Augustine made it known in northern Africa. The monk called St. Martin of Tours took it to Gaul.

Martin of Tours (c.316–397)

Martin was born in Szombathely (Hungary) where his father, a Roman soldier, was stationed. A considerable amount is known about Martin from the hagiography his friend Sulpicius Severus wrote. He converted to Christianity when he was ten. After a stint in the Roman army, he lived as a hermit for some time before making his way to France. There he became a disciple of Hilary, the bishop of Poitiers, joining the fight against Arianism. Martin traveled to Italy, but returned to found Gaul's first monastery in Ligugé. He was appointed bishop of Tours in 371, a decision he objected to but obeyed. He established another monastery in Marmoutier, following the cenobitic model of his first one. Severus attributes a number of miracles to him and describes his giving half of his cloak to a beggar at Amiens that led to a vision of Christ. Famous for his missionary work in the country, he is the patron saint of France.

John Cassian (360–435)

The theologian John Cassian (also called Johannes Eremita or Johannes Massiliensis) lived fifteen years as a desert hermit in Egypt prior to becoming a priest. About 415 he founded two monasteries (Sts. Peter and Victor) for men and one (St. Savior) for women in Marseilles (France). The name by which he is known, Lawgiver of Monastic Life, is justified. Cassian wrote works on the life of monks describing spiritual exercise and the practical problems that arise inside a monastic community. He opposed Augustine's notion of humankind's inheritance of original sin from Adam and his concepts of unearned grace and moral choice in salvation. He also wrote a well-reasoned treatise against Nestorian theology that denied Jesus' divinity.

St. Jerome (c.345–420)

Jerome, born in Stridon near the Roman province of Dalmatia, was sent to Rome to

Central altarpiece from the cathedral of Grasse (France), with a portrait of Honoratus, bishop of Arles

Hieronymus departs
from Rome to go and settle
in Bethlehem. Miniature from
a ninth-century Bible

study. He became familiar with both pagan and Christian literature and fluent in Latin, Greek, and Hebrew. He then withdrew to the desert, living as an ascetic and continuing to study the scriptures. In 379 he returned to be ordained and spent the next three years with the theologian Gregory of Nazianzus in Constantinople. He was made secretary to Pope Damasus I in 382. In Rome he converted a number of Roman aristocrats, including many women. Two of them, the widow Paula (later St. Paula) and her daughter followed him to Bethlehem in 385, where they founded three convents for women and another for men, run by Jerome. There Jerome fought passionate theological battles within and without the Church. Writing as Eusebius Hieronymus, he translated the Bible into Latin. Recognized by the ecumenical Council of Trent, it was called the Vulgate (meaning "widely distributed") and used by the Roman Catholic church for centuries.

St. Benedict of Nursia (c.480–c.547)
Benedict, called the father of Western monasticism for his rules of monastic life, was born to a prominent family in the hamlet of Nursia in Umbria (Italy). He was sent to Rome for his studies, but found the city so degenerate that he retreated to a cave (later called the Holy Grotto) near Subiaco. He stayed there for three years, gaining a reputation for saintliness and visited by crowds of people. Accepting the invitation of some monks to become their abbot, he subsequently provoked the resident prelate. Learning of a plot to poison him, he left and established a monastery on Mount Cassino. An ancient temple to Apollo supplied its building mate-

rials. Benedict lived there the rest of his days. He wrote a set of monastic rules of such practical use that most Western monasteries would subsequently adopt them. He stressed communal living, physical labor, communal property and meals, and the avoidance of unnecessary speech.

"Hearken, children," Benedict begins, "to the voice of the master and rejoice in receiving the exhortations of a pious father, so that thou mayest return in obedience to Him from whom thou hast parted through negligence or rebelliousness." He follows this with several pieces of advice: "He who remembers that the word *abbot* means father and proves this through his actions shall be worthy of ruling a monastery. He must be just, righteous, strict, and competent. He must be able to teach God's commandments with the aid of the holy scriptures. Through his example he shall guide those less studied to the way of the Lord." The abbot must "correct, condemn, exhort. In cases of extraordinary rebelliousness, he shall even wield the cane."

Benedict offers even less discussion of democracy than Basil did in his monastic regulations. Though the abbot must consult the monks in certain matters, "he, after hearing the views of his brethren, must decide as he deems fit. On the other hand, all monks must be called, because sometimes the Lord

Detail of a Byzantine panel >
depicting the death of Ephrem
Syrus, a church father and
poet from Syria. In this detail
monks can be seen at work,
during prayer, meditating,
and teaching.

ΗΤΧΑΣΧΕΦΡΑΙΜΟΥΡΟΥ

977

reveals himself to the youngest, which is the most suitable for the community." That same community meeting is to elect the abbot. "In the event the meeting elects an incompetent abbot, the bishop of the diocese where the monastery is located or the abbots of the neighboring monasteries shall appoint an overseer worthy of ruling the house of God."

Regarding the way of life that would lead to the kingdom of God, Benedict's recommendation was as short as it was clear: *ora et labora* (pray and work). He specified the religious exercises the monks had to complete daily, including the kind of chants they were to use. Later called Gregorian chants, these had to be simple melodies sung in unison, not harmonies of several parts.

Benedict forbade all personal property. Monks were not allowed to have their own cell. They slept in large dormitories, where at least one candle was always lit. Their meal consisted of two light dishes. If apples and vegetables were available, these had to be added to the food. Meat was a privilege Benedict allowed only for the weak and the sick. Somewhat reluctantly, he granted his monks a half pint of wine per day. "But those who abstain shall reap their reward." He meticulously laid out the working hours for both summer and winter. If there were artists, Benedict adds emphatically, "They must be allowed to continue their work, if they do so humbly." The artworks were sold on the monastery's behalf, but their price would be lower than was customary for those made by artists in the secular world, "so that God may be glorified in them, as in all things."

The Benedictine monks lived in what could be called sensible simplicity and piety, at no point moving beyond the boundaries of the tolerable into the ascetic excesses of fanaticism. He permitted the monasteries to grant the culture of ancient Greece and Rome a place in their libraries. "All reasonable men will agree that knowledge of all matters within our reach is the most important. And here I do not mean the knowledge that is loftier, such as ours (that is, the knowledge of God), but I mean external knowledge which many Christians despise as being perfidious, harmful, and likely to move us away from God. It is knowing that deserves to be condemned, some would like to say; those who argue this way, on the contrary, are blind and unknowing, and want the entire world to resemble them so as to hide their personal shortcomings in the mass of people."

St. Martin of Tours on a panel made in the thirteenth century. Around him are pictures of important events from his life—on the left, his most famous deed: He cuts his cloak in half in order to share it with a beggar.

Carolingian miniature depicting Gregory the Great preparing a sermon. The Holy Spirit, here depicted as a dove, gives him inspiration. According to a legend, his secretary saw this scene one time when he opened the curtain behind which Gregory was working.

The Church in the West

The Christianization of Europe

Christianity, once persecuted in the Roman Empire, was decreed legal by Constantine in 313 and then made the state religion. Subsequent emperors tried to bring the Church under their control and used it to justify their deeds. They organized councils, manipulated episcopal appointments, and vigorously espoused various theological causes. The Church resisted this imperial interference where possible. In Rome, it was increasingly possible. Constantine's establishment of Byzantium (which he renamed Constantinople) as his capital in 330 gradually reduced Rome, the Eternal City, to a provincial capital. By the end of the fourth century, the papacy was relatively free of restraints and the pope was the most important man in Rome. The last Roman emperor fell in 476, leaving the Church essentially free to control western Europe. In the fifth century, it was not civil authority but Pope Leo the Great who saved the city from the ravages of Attila the Hun. As the empire divided, the citizens of Rome began to

Gregory the Great prays for a monk who has broken his vow of poverty and has therefore been sent to purgatory. This helps, and the sinner is freed by two angels. The relief dates from the fifteenth century.

accord the papacy far more authority than the weakened imperial remnants in Ravenna or the far-off emperor in Constantinople.

In the East, there was no such crisis of imperial authority. The Eastern Roman emperors managed to protect the empire against the storms of migrating tribes. Almost all the emperors were enthusiastic amateur theologians who shaped the faith for both spiritual and political reasons. In Constantinople, the Church was far from the independent force it was in Rome. Caesaropapism, the special relationship between Church and State, became the norm. The patriarch of the Church was increasingly a tool in the hands of the imperial establishment, a sacred ornament at the Bronze Palace. Eastern Christians took their cue from Constantinople. Rome was far away, another culture, where the people spoke

Latin rather than Greek. A major issue was the claim of the Monophysites that Jesus Christ possessed only a single, divine nature.

The Council of Chalcedon (451)

Eastern Emperor Marcian convoked the fourth ecumenical council at Chalcedon on October 8, 451, to overturn the decisions of the earlier "Robber Synod" of Ephesus that had upheld the Monophysite view. Running until November 1, the council condemned Monophysitism (also called Eutychianism). Pope Leo wrote a *Tome to Flavian* (the bishop of Constantinople), asserting Rome's opinion in the Chalcedonian Definition. The West accepted twenty-seven canons of the council on ecclesiastical administration but rejected at least one. It would have granted the bishop of Constantinople the title of patriarch, giving him equal status with the pope. Asserting the primacy of the pope, the council marked the first major schism between the churches.

Germanic Migration

Italy, the last bulwark of the Western Roman Empire, fell into the hands of German invaders in the early fifth century AD. For almost a century, devastating wars imperiled the city of Rome. Emperor Justinian's occupation of Italy in the sixth century did not last long. Not ten years after his death, the Lombards crossed the Alps to the fertile Italian plains, bringing their wives and children and all their possessions. An exhausted Constantinople was unable to organize any effective resistance. The soldiers retreated to small bridgeheads throughout the country, while the Lombards established their dukedoms. The Byzantine islands in Lombard (Italy) became virtually independent states. The Eastern emperor was satisfied if governors simply swore their loyalty and paid nominal tribute.

The Ecclesiastical State

One of these political islands was Rome. Power there was exercised by a city prefect. Ranking just below him was the pope. He performed the traditional tasks of a bishop, which had not been exclusively religious for a long time. Christians had traditionally referred legal conflicts to their spiritual leaders for decision. The pope was thus also a judge, which gave him considerable influence. As political power gradually concentrated in the papal palace, the emperor in Constantinople made no protest. As the local political power of the popes grew, their religious influence waned elsewhere, apart from turbulent Italy. It appeared they might decline to the status of regional princes when

this trend was brought to a halt by Pope Gregory the Great, the first spiritual leader listened to throughout the world.

Gregory I (the Great) (c.540–604)

Pope Gregory I was descended from an ancient Roman family. His background alone ensured him a brilliant career. His grandfather Felix III had served as pope from 483 to 492. In 570, Gregory became city prefect of Rome with no great effort. To everyone's surprise, he distinguished himself by fairness rather than the more common corruption. People were even more surprised when he withdrew from the world to dedicate his life in silence to God. In 575, he turned his family estate into a monastery, attracting the notice of the papal palace. Pope Pelagius II, taking office in 579, appointed Gregory as his representative to the imperial court in Constantinople the same year. Upon the death of Pelagius in 590, Gregory was elected pope.

A very pragmatic shepherd with significant talents as an administrator, Gregory led his flock through it all, enhancing the prestige of the papacy both regionally and internationally. As soon as he took office, Gregory reorganized papal administration by appointing an assistant, the *vice-dominus* (or "underlord"), responsible for supervising routine tasks and keeping the wheels of the papal economy turning. Part of his task was the management of the *Patrimonium Petri* (Inheritance of Peter).

This was land acquired over the course of centuries by the papacy. Those outside Rome were managed by rent collectors. The popes used the income from this *Patrimonium Petri* to pay their own living expenses and

The church of Saints Cosmus and Damian in Rome is one of the earliest Christian churches. In this photograph, its tower stands out on the left. The Forum Romanum is in the foreground and the Colosseum is visible in the background.

those of the Church. Gregory had this real estate effectively exploited, as evidenced by the letters he wrote to his rent collectors.

But the pope was still not free to devote himself peacefully to his pastoral tasks. In 594 the Arian Lombards were threatening the city gates. Despite his requests to Constantinople, no aid against the invading Lombards had come. He set up a citizens' patrol and had the crumbling city walls repaired as well as possible. He bought weapons for his citizen army with income from the *Patrimonium Petri* and confidently assured the troops that God was standing behind them with his own troops of martyrs and angels. Rome appeared more formidable, and the Lombards concluded that the Eternal City would not be easy prey. Gregory negotiated with them himself, preventing their sacking of Rome by agreeing to pay a yearly tribute. The Lombards accepted.

Rome then withdrew its protection from the Byzantine enclaves in Italy. The court in Constantinople was furious. The pope, acting as the unofficial governor of Rome, had clearly shown that he was, in fact, its capable sovereign. The emperor could do no more against this annoying pope than he could against the Lombards, but in Rome Gregory was more popular than ever. The citizens were made aware every day that their city was ruled by a man of God, who had finally brought peace to his flock. Gregory put a stop to the profane entertainments that the Byzantine imperial establishment was still offering to the rest of the Roman Empire. The pope organized no more chariot races for his 30,000 subjects. In their place he held awe-inspiring religious services in the city's mighty basilicas.

Buckle of a richly decorated Longobard sword belt from the sixth century

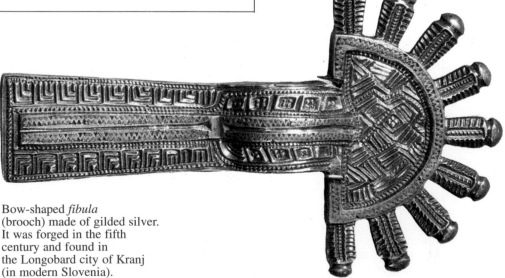

Bow-shaped *fibula* (brooch) made of gilded silver. It was forged in the fifth century and found in the Longobard city of Kranj (in modern Slovenia).

Gregorian Chants

The pope eliminated laymen from the choirs, declaring that only the clergy were to sing the sacred songs. He took an active interest in collecting Roman chants and in the quality of the chorales to be performed and made them a part of the worship service. The Roman Catholic Church today still officially recognizes only this music, referred to as Gregorian in his honor. It consists of undu-

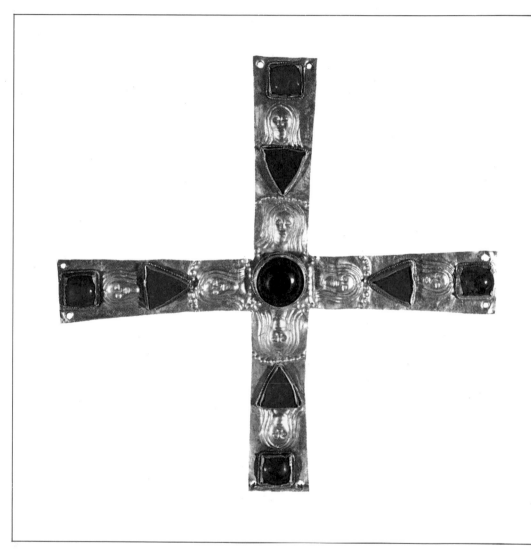

lating tones with no fixed rhythm, monoharmonic (with a single melodic line) rather than polyharmonic. Some 3,000 Gregorian chants are known.

Gregory's Writings

Gregory was convinced of the doctrine of papal supremacy. He operated cautiously, made no unnecessary enemies, and concealed his keenness beneath great amiability.

Longobard cross (sixth century) that was worn on the chest. It is made of gold and decorated with precious stones.

Statue of Gregory the Great from the church in Rome that is dedicated to him

Part of a Byzantine altar cloth from the seventh century

St. Bede
(673–735)

In many ways, the learned monk Bede symbolized the change that occurred in England over his own lifetime. New ties through the Church linked Britain with Europe and Rome. Only a century earlier Roman Catholic Christianity had reached southeast England through Augustine of Canterbury, but the faith spread rapidly. Benedict Biscop founded the monastery of Wearmouth in northern England shortly after Bede was born. Benedict Theodorus had brought books, relics, and art treasures from the continent and Benedict set up a valuable library in his monastery.

In 680, the seven-year-old Bede was entrusted to the care of a scholarly abbot by his parents. Two years later, when a monastery was founded in Jarrow as an offshoot of Wearmouth, the boy moved to the new establishment.

The connections Benedict and Archbishop Theodorus had with Rome resulted in a flow of fresh inspiration to the monasteries. The young Bede studied Greek and learned Gregorian chant. An anonymous but undisputed historic report, *The Life of Abbot Ceolfrid*, describes the monastery in Jarrow once afflicted by a plague. All the monks died but the abbot and a young boy he was bringing up. The boy must have been Bede, although the name is not mentioned. As a result of this disaster, the abbot could no longer have the Latin psalms performed antiphonally—that is, by two choirs responding to one another—because he and the young Bede were the only singers. Nevertheless, they sang vespers and matins (the evening and morning prayers) in this manner. However, after a week, Ceolfrid began, with Bede, to train newcomers in the sacred songs.

Bede spent his entire life at Jarrow. While still a young man, he became a deacon and later a priest. Stimulated by his surroundings, he became a great scholar, using his gifts to write commentaries on various books of the Bible, biographies of holy abbots, and the colorful *Historia ecclesiastica gentis Anglorum* (*Ecclesiastical History of the English People*). He portrayed the Church as a force for civilization, forging a godly and

In the West, respect for him steadily increased, and eventually he was recognized by all the bishops. In order to clarify their rights and duties, he wrote a brief treatise, the *Regula pastoralis*, and *Liber Pastoralis Curae* (*Pastoral Care*). In particular, Gregory denounced the widespread evil of simony, the practice of selling church offices to the highest bidder. The book was even translated into Greek for readers in the East, an indication of the prestige that the Holy See was acquiring.

At about the same time, Gregory com-

984

educational culture in a barbaric world. He collected data, written and oral, organizing it in a manner that would form a model for future historians in Europe.

Bede lived and worked at a time when England was being Christianized and Anglo-Saxon missionaries worked on the continent to win heathen areas for the faith. It was also a time of Islamic conquest in the east and south. The Muslims seized Christian territory as far as southern Gaul. The Islamic advance was halted by the Franks at Poitiers in 732, a year after Bede had completed his history.

Miniature from a manuscript describing the life of St. Cuthbert. It depicts a monk, probably Bede, at his writing desk.

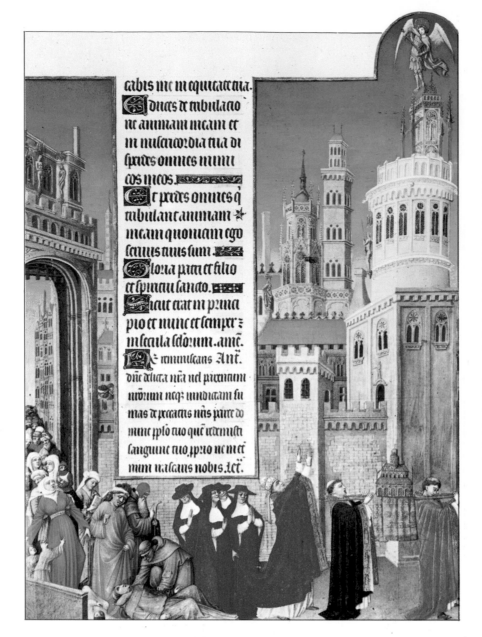

posed a theological treatise at the urging of a Spanish bishop. Titled *Moralia in Job* (*Morals on the Book of Job*), it is a detailed commentary on the doctrines of the book of Job.

In *Dialogues*, Gregory wrote stories of the saints around him, notably the hagiography (biography of a saint) of St. Benedict.

The pope also delivered a series of sermons on the many calamities that Rome suffered during his pontificate. He propagated a Christianity designed for the poor layman, a religion full of miracles, angels, devils, sin, and conversion, with eternal salvation shining on the horizon for the righteous. He wrote a great many letters that were collected into fourteen books that broaden our understanding of the man and the era. Noted above all for his pastoral attitude, he expressed great concern for the souls of heathens and heretics.

The Conversion of the Angles and Saxons
There is a story that Gregory, passing through the slave market in Rome, was impressed by the proud appearance of the recently imported slaves. They told him that they were Angles (people from Britain). "Well, then," replied the pope, "we shall make these Angles into angels!"

Whether or not the tale is factual, Gregory initiated a second great wave of conversion of Britains to Christianity. The large number of pagans living within the former Roman province had weakened the influence of the Church, with the few Christians converted in the fourth century swept away by the flood of tribes that had overrun the island. In 597

Gregory the Great prays for the cure of a monk who has fallen victim to the plague. Decorated page from a manuscript that dates from the fifteenth century

A scene from the life of Gregory the Great. Here he celebrates a mass and thus liberates the souls of dead people from purgatory.

Gregory behind his writing desk. At the bottom, monks are busy copying manuscripts. Ivory relief from the tenth century

Angles into angels was Augustine, an energetic Roman Benedictine later canonized as St. Augustine of Canterbury. With a group of monks, he traveled first to Aix-en-Provence (France). They were all so intimidated by stories of the savage British islanders that they returned to Rome and asked Gregory to

Gregory sent Augustine, the abbot of his own monastery of St. Andrew, and forty monks to the king of the Jutes in Canterbury (Britain). The mission was highly successful, evolving into a conversion campaign throughout the northern European continent and greatly strengthening the position of the papacy.

Gregory died on March 12, 604. His subsequent canonization is said to have been the result of popular demand. Subsequent generations would call him Gregory the Great. Over the fourteen years of his pontificate he had breathed new life into the Church. The Holy See, surrounded by loyal subjects in Italy, now commanded international respect.

In 1298, Pope Gregory I was named a Doctor of the Church. Taken from the Latin *doctor ecclesiae*, the title is awarded only to canonized saints who are distinguished scholars and have made outstanding contributions to Christian theology and the understanding of doctrine. Gregory was one of the original four Western Doctors of the Church. The others were the theologians and saints Ambrose, Augustine, and Jerome, all also named in 1298. Saint Thomas Aquinas was given the title in 1568. Saints Athanasius, Basil, John Chrysostom, and Gregory of Nazianzus were named as Eastern Doctors of the Church the same year. Saints Catherine of Siena and Teresa of Ávila, the first women granted the title, were named in 1970.

St. Augustine of Canterbury (died c.604)
The man who had the job of turning the

Statue of St. Patrick, the man who converted the Irish people to Christianity in the fifth century

let them give up the effort. He said no. Reluctantly they headed back to Canterbury, center of the kingdom of Kent, established by the people called Jutes a century earlier. The pagan Kentish king Ethelbert had married Bertha, a Christian Frankish princess. At the intercession of the queen, Augustine and his companions were well received in Kent, where the Benedictines appear to have had greater persuasive power than the princess. On June 2, 597, the king of Kent agreed to baptism. The event accelerated the pace of popular conversion. Augustine was made the first archbishop of Canterbury and given authority over future bishops in Britain.

He had competition from both the Christian and the pagan Celts in Ireland. The country had never been part of the Roman Empire. The Celts who lived there still clung to their old traditions, their Celtic tongue, and the wars endemic to their society. Long before Augustine set foot in Kent, Christianity had made significant inroads in that culture. In the fifth century the monk Patrick had preached the Christian faith there with such success that Ireland became a permanent Christian outpost in a pagan world. Celtic Christians had virtually no contact with Christians elsewhere. As a result, a unique Celtic faith arose, radically different in structure from that instituted by Gregory. The Irish Church was organized around monasteries rather than around the church hierarchy in Rome. Throughout the country were rigorous orders where monks strove to gain the kingdom of heaven through asceticism, and peasants from the surrounding area came in droves to hear mass and view the gigantic "high crosses" with scenes from the Bible carved in stone. As early as the sixth century the Irish monasteries had become centers of culture. In their libraries, monks studied the old texts and made new copies of them. While Augustine was working on the conversion of Kent, Celtic monks were disseminating their own form of Christianity in the north of England. About 603 Augustine attempted to unify the Celtic and Roman liturgy and practices. The Irish would have no part of it. In 634, they established a monastery in Lindisfarne that was to develop into one of the most prestigious cultural centers of Europe. About the same time, Roman Christians founded a school in the southern archbishopric of Canterbury where people could study Greek, Roman law, art, and literature. It was considered a bridgehead of culture.

The Anglo-Saxons in Britain knew of far-off Rome and of Constantinople, a marvel even more remote. They began to travel to see these wonders for themselves, many of them making pilgrimages to papal Rome. What the Romans regarded as a city of ruins filled the pilgrims with awe. About 30,000 people still lived there, an enormous number

The church of
Santa Sabina in Rome, which
was built in the first half
of the fifth century

The Ogham stone in
county Kerry, Ireland. It was
erected in the first century
AD. People believed
that it would keep the soul of
a dead person forever.

Illuminated page from the
so-called Lindisfarne Gospels.
The book was written in the seventh
century and is one of the most
beautiful and best preserved
of the period.

989

to average Britons who were used to the rural villages of their own country. Full of admiration, they returned home to try to re-create what they had seen abroad.

Roman influence in Britain grew, coming into conflict with the Celtic. A major bone of

Early Christian gravestone from England (fifth century). The inscription is in Greek.

contention between the two groups of Christians was the date of Easter. The Celts had their own method of computation that differed from the one used in Canterbury. There, Christians based the date on Roman standards. The question was resolved in 664 when the Synod of Whitby adopted the Roman Easter only after fierce argument.

There was another major dispute over the forms of ecclesiastical organization. In Britain the Roman type of episcopal hierarchy prevailed, while in Ireland the dioceses were set up around the monasteries.

St. Bede the Venerable (c.673–735)

The Anglo-Saxon monastic culture reached a high point in the early eighth century with the British-born Benedictine monk called the Venerable Bede. Sent to the monastery of Wearmouth and Jarrow in Northumbria at the age of seven (a common practice at the time), he lived there the rest of his life. His knowledge of Greek and Latin gave him access to the extensive literature available by then in England. He wrote some forty works that included theological treatises (one criticizing aspects of the Vulgate, St. Jerome's Latin translation of the Bible), hagiographies, and biographies of abbots in his own monastery (*Historia abbatum*, c.725). His major work was *Historia ecclesiastica gentis Anglorum* (*Ecclesiastical History of the English People*), which was important to English history from Roman occupation to 731, the year he completed the book. In *De Temporum ratione* (*On the Reckoning of Time*, 725) he introduced the concept of dating events by their position in time before or after the birth of Christ. He used AD (*Anno domini*; the year of the Lord) and BC (before Christ). The practice had already taken root in the East by the sixth century, introduced by the monk Dionysius Exiguus. Bede was canonized in 1899.

Anglo-Saxon Missionary Efforts in Europe

As the seventh century began, the only orthodox country of importance in Europe was the Frankish kingdom of Clovis's successors. It had expanded across the Rhine and become a constant threat to the Friesians living along the shores of the North Sea. It was understandable that the Friesians were reluctant to welcome Frankish missionaries. Now they faced Anglo-Saxons landing on the coast from England, preachers from a different direction advocating the same faith as the Franks. Usually accompanied by twelve companions, they posed no threat of territorial conquest. Their land lay across the sea and was of no political significance. Moreover, their language was almost the same as that of the Friesians.

The new missionaries traveled the country, founding monasteries on the Irish model. The most famous of these eighth-century missionaries from Britain were Willibrord, known as the Apostle of the Netherlands, and Boniface, the Apostle of Germany.

TIME LINE

INDIA, BUDDHISM, AND HINDUISM POLITICAL HISTORY	INDIA, BUDDHISM, AND HINDUISM CULTURAL HISTORY	EVENTS IN THE REST OF THE WORLD

BC

2000

c.2000 Indus Valley civilization
c.2000–1900 First Indo-European peoples reach the Valley of the Indus; raids by mountain peoples from the north weaken the cities
c.1800 End of the Indus Valley civilization

1800

c.1800 Diffusion of Indo-Aryan culture; introduction of the caste system
c.1800–1200 In the Punjab, a series of hymns —the *Rig-Veda*—is composed, to be recited while making offerings; the religion is dominated by the priests or Brahmans; Brahmanism is a kind of public religion in which the gods of heaven are worshiped

900

c.880–660 *Brahmanas*, books explaining the hymns and their ritual application
800–500 The *Aranyakas* and *Upanishads* teach the inner meaning of offerings; emergence of a personal religion with an increasing number of female gods, in addition to the rise of ascetic movements (Buddhism and Jainism)

800

700

600

c.600–400 Flowering of cities and trade, introduction of coined money and the written alphabet; use of iron; emergence of specialized sciences; religious unrest; new religious movements compete with Brahmanism

500

c.500 The Indian subcontinent approaches cultural homogeneity; contact with other cultures, including Iran, the Persian Empire, and China; unity is promoted by Brahmanism
480–400 The Buddha, Siddhartha Gautama, announces his new "teaching of the eightfold path"; Buddhism denies that man has a soul, Buddha's teachings become a healing method

551–479 Confucius (Kong Fuzi)

513 India pays tribute to the Persians

400

c.400 BC–AD 200 *The Mahabharata*, the epic describing the battle among Bharata's descendants
c.373 Buddhist councils argue about monastic rules; peace cannot be restored; schisms and formation of sects

372–279 Mencius (Mengzi)

327 Alexander the Great in the Punjab
325 Greek troops withdraw westward
324 Chandragupta establishes his power in the Punjab, dynasty of the Mauryas

300

c.270 Asoka is king of the entire Indian subcontinent
269 Bloody conquest of the region of Kalinga and consequent conversion of Asoka to Buddhism

269 Asoka rules as a humane monarch, encouraging proselytizing activities. Thanks to his efforts, Buddhism becomes a mass movement

c.250 Buddhism established in Sri Lanka

232 Death of Asoka

200

c.200 Composition of the *Bhagavad-Gita*, one of the holiest poems of Hinduism

c.200–50 Buddhism penetrates as far as the eastern Greek kingdoms, especially Bactria

150

c.150 *Yoga* of Patanjali

Prehistory	Antiquity	Middle Ages	Renaissance	Modern History	Contemporary History

INDIA, BUDDHISM, AND HINDUISM POLITICAL HISTORY	INDIA, BUDDHISM, AND HINDUISM CULTURAL HISTORY	EVENTS IN THE REST OF THE WORLD
	c.100–50 *Mahayana*, "the great Vehicle," new teachings in Buddhism, presented as a separate revelation by the Buddha, with a devotional trend and a philosophical and scholastic movement **c.100–0** The *Ramayana*	**c.100** Blending of Confucianism with Daoism
	c.200–1500 The *Purana*, an encyclopedic work	**c.220–280** Buddhist monks settle in China and spread Buddhism
320–499 Nearly all of northern India is ruled by the Gupta dynasty	**c.300–400** Cultural flowering, golden age of Buddhism and Brahmanism	**c.350** Chinese influence in Japan and Korea
	c.400 Popularity of the worship of Shakti, the Great Goddess	**c.350–850** Buddhism spreads in southeast Asia
500–1300 The southern and central parts of India are ruled by rivaling dynasties	**c.500–700** Buddhism is slowly forced out of southern and western India **c.550** Tantrism develops on the basis of texts and books, the *Kama Sutra* is written	**c.550** Tantrism, a mystical trend arises within the Mahayana in Tibet
600–1000 Rajput dynasty rules in northwestern India **600–1200** Pala/sena dynasty in Bengal **606–647** Empire of Harsha		**c.552** Monks introduce Buddhism in Japan **c.600** Foundation of the kingdom of Tibet, in regions of western China
712 Beginning of Islamic influence on India		
	788–820 The great thinker Shankara believes only in the existence of Brahma, the divine Absolute	**c.800** Tibet declines politically; Lamaism, a typical Tibetan form of Buddhism, evolves
1001 Muslims occupy the Punjab		
1192 Muhammad of Ghur conquers the Hindu kingdom of Delhi **1200** Islamic Turks conquer all of northern India; Buddhism is relegated to a few peripheral areas	**1137** Death of Ramanuja, founder of a pantheistic trend within Hinduism **1199–1278** Madhva believes the soul exists independent of a supreme being	
	1479–1531 Vallabha teaches that the world is only a phenomenon in the eyes of the beholder	

BC 100 · 0 · AD 200 · 300 · 400 · 500 · 600 · 700 · 800 · 900 · 1000 · 1100 · 1200 · 1300 · 1400 · 1500

| Prehistory | Antiquity | Middle Ages | Renaissance | Modern History | Contemporary History |

CHINA POLITICAL HISTORY	CHINA CULTURAL HISTORY	EVENTS IN THE REST OF THE WORLD
1027 The Zhou dynasty conquers the Shang dynasty	**c.1000** The legendary Golden Age, when people knew the right path, according to Confucius who taught that it is possible to rediscover the right path again through the study of history	**753** Legendary founding of Rome by Romulus **660** Legendary founding of the state of Japan
	c.600–400 The ideal of Daoism is to allow matters to run their natural course, leaving the old unchanged; everything exists only by virtue of its opposite is a Daoist belief	**586–537** Babylonian captivity of the Jewish people **c.550** Phoenicians sail around Africa
c.500 During the Zhou dynasty, China declines politically	**551–479** Kong Fuzi (Confucius or Master Kong), a political thinker **c.500** Confucius breaks new ground in humanism and rationalism, arguing that everyone must work for a better world without appealing to the supernatural; he emphasizes secular, humanistic ethics **c.500** Legendary figure of Laozi (Old Master)	
480–221 Warring States period **c.450** First written laws in China; army converted into an army of farmers	**480–221** Despite civil war, this is a flourishing period with population growth, increase in trade, coined money, expansion of the cities, and the search by philosophers for an ideology of reform for the state; increasing interest in legalism, a rationalist state philosophy of government	**480–400** The Buddha and his teachings in India
	372–289 According to Mengzi (Mencius) restoration of the empire is possible only through the virtue of the ruler, and people are good through their own natures **369–286** Zhuangzi, an important representative of Daoism, makes her ideas accessible to a wide audience	**334–323** Alexander the Great establishes a world empire
221–206 Qin, having become the most powerful state, supplies the first emperor, Qin Shihuangdi **220–207** Power struggle; the empire continues to exist	**c.250** *Daode Jing*, the holy book of the Path and its Virtue, is attributed to Laozi **221–206** Two legalists, Li Si and Han Fei, are advisers to the first emperor **213** Burning of Confucianist works	**270** Asoka rules a large part of India **c.250** Buddhism established in Sri Lanka
202 BC–AD 220 Han dynasty	**c.200** Compilation of the *Lunyu (Analects)*, a compilation of the sayings of Confucius **124** Founding of an official Confucian academy **100** Blending of Confucianism and Daoism	**c.200** The Septuagint translation of the Bible into Greek **167** Uprising of the Maccabees in Palestine **c.100** The *Mahayana* is a new trend in Buddhism
		22 Restoration of the Han dynasty in China **64** Great fire of Rome; first persecutions of Christians **70** Destruction of the Temple in Jerusalem
	c.100 Buddhism in China	
	c.250 Confucianism is reinterpreted	
	c.350 Buddhism penetrates to the emperor's court	
		410 Goths led by Alaric plunder Rome **500–600** Tantrism in Tibet
		c.552 Monks introduce Buddhism to Japan **553** Conquest of Italy by Justinian
618–907 Tang dynasty	**618–907** Confucianism again becomes the philosophy of a majority	**731** Bede's *Historia Ecclesiastica Gentis Anglorum* **800** Charlemagne crowned emperor in Rome
	c.850 Decline and persecution of Buddhism, followed by the rise of Daoism	

BC 1000 / 700 / 600 / 500 / 400 / 300 / 200 / 100 / 0 / AD / 100 / 200 / 300 / 400 / 500 / 600 / 700 / 800 / 900

| Prehistory | Antiquity | Middle Ages | Renaissance | Modern History | Contemporary History |

THE JEWISH PEOPLE POLITICAL HISTORY	THE JEWISH PEOPLE CULTURAL HISTORY	EVENTS IN THE REST OF THE WORLD
587 Nebuchadnezzar deports the elite of conquered Judah to Babylon **587–536** Babylonian captivity	**587–536** The Jews succeed in preserving their own identity; intensification of the faith by prophets; Jahweh becomes a universal god; great emphasis on salvation through a Messiah; the ancient prophecies are recorded	
536 Cyrus conquers the New Babylonian Empire and allows the Jews to return home; Persians support the colonists	**536** The first 40,000 families depart for Palestine; the Temple in Jerusalem is rebuilt	**551–479** Confucius (Kong Fuzi) **509** Foundation of the Roman Republic **480–221** Warring States period in China **480–400** The Buddha **478/7** The foundation of the Delian League
457 The priest Ezra brings 1,800 of the faithful to Jerusalem **444** Nehemiah arrives with a new group of believers	**457** Ezra, scholar of the law, institutes religious reforms **444** Nehemiah brings documents granting autonomy to the Jews and organizes the civil administration; together with Ezra, he reads the Law to the people	
332 Alexander the Great conquers Palestine and adopts the Persians' policies toward the Jews **323** Death of Alexander the Great; Palestine in the hands of Ptolemy of Egypt, who continues traditional policies	**323** Many Jews move to Alexandria, where they come in contact with Hellenistic ideas	**372–289** Mencius (Mengzi) **334–323** Alexander the Great conquers a world empire **270** Asoka rules a large part of India **202** Beginning of the Han dynasty in China
	c.200 The *Septuagint*, translation of the Bible into Greek	**c.200** Composition of the *Bhagavad-Gita*, one of the most sacred poems of Hinduism
198 The Syrian Antiochus conquers the Ptolemies' possessions in Palestine **188** Antiochus pays tribute to Rome	**198–188** Antiochus begins an active policy of Hellenization and tries to fill his empty treasury; increasing interference from Antioch, differentiation between prominent Jews who adopt Greek names and standards and the common people who live according to the ancient traditions	
167 After a violent revolt in Jerusalem, Antiochus IV Epiphanes interferes, causing a massacre; revolt of the Maccabees; guerilla warfare by the priest Mattathias and his sons against Syrian rule **167–160** Judas Maccabaeus frees the majority of Palestine **140** Maccabees conquer Jerusalem; Palestine becomes a monarchy ruled by the Maccabees	**167** King Antiochus IV personally takes charge of the Hellenization process, announcing that the Jewish religion must be eradicated **138** Simon coins the first Jewish money	**124** Foundation of an official Confucian academy **100** Blending of Confucianism and Taoism
63 The Roman general Pompey brings Palestine within the Roman sphere of influence **25–4** Herod the Great rules as king of Palestine under Roman protection **4** After Herod's death, the empire is divided among his sons	**c.100 BC–AD 66** Essenes withdraw from everyday life; *Dead Sea Scrolls* **25–4** Herod treats the Jews severely, favoring the pagans; impoverishment of the populace	**c.6** Birth of Jesus in Bethlehem
4 Archelaus is deposed and the coastal region of Palestine is placed under Syrian rule **4–66** Resistance against the Romans	**4–66** Zealots advocate resistance against the Romans	**c.30** Crucifixion of Jesus at Jerusalem **54** First epistle of Paul to the Corinthians
66–70 Jewish uprising against Rome; radical elements seize power in Jerusalem; Vespasian and Titus restore order	**70** The Temple in Jerusalem is destroyed; beginning of the Diaspora; the rabbis keep faith in the coming of the Messiah	**64** Great fire of Rome; first persecutions of Christians

BC 600 — 500 — 400 — 300 — 200 — 100 — 0 — AD — 50 — 100

| Prehistory | Antiquity | Middle Ages | Renaissance | Modern History | Contemporary History |

CHRISTIANITY POLITICAL HISTORY	CHRISTIANITY CULTURAL HISTORY	EVENTS IN THE REST OF THE WORLD
BC		
25–4 Herod ruled as king of Judaea	**25–4** John the Baptist announces that the Kingdom of God is approaching and baptizes his followers	
	c.27–AD 30 Jesus preaches among the people; miracles and healings reinforce the power of his words; his teachings gain him a large following, including the twelve apostles; he is called the Messiah or Anointed	
c.6 Jesus is born in Bethlehem, the son of very simple parents		
AD		
c.30 Jesus is crucified at Jerusalem	**c.30** Jesus preaches in the courtyard of the Temple in Jerusalem; three days after his death he is said to appear to his disciples; in Jerusalem and surrounding areas, communities of Jesus' followers arise; they have communal property and they are persecuted	**22** Restoration of the Han dynasty after the end of the Wang Mang rebellion
	c.40 Jesus' followers call themselves Christians and increasingly diverge from traditional Judaism; Paul becomes the greatest proselytizer of the new religion outside of Palestine	
	50 Deacons assume some of the tasks of the apostles, especially caring for the poor	
54–68 Nero is emperor of Rome	**54** First epistle of Paul to the Corinthians	
	60 Various communities of Christians arise in Rome	
64 Great fire of Rome unleashes the first persecutions of Christians	**64** Death of Peter in Rome during the first persecutions	**66–70** Jewish revolt in Palestine
	67 Death of apostle Paul	**70** Destruction of the Temple in Jerusalem
	70 St. Mark writes his gospel	
	70–100 The Gospel according to Luke	
	90 Compilation of the gospels	
98–117 The emperor Trajan prohibits active searches for Christians	**c.100** The Gospel according to St. John	**c.100** Paper is invented in China
	c.100–200 Christianity spreads in the eastern parts of the Roman Empire; a centralized structure is lacking; persecutions are the exception, martyrs are venerated	
	c.150 Vast popularity of Mary and veneration of angels	**c.150** Teotihuacán emerges as a state in Central America
	156 Persecution of the Christians in Smyrna; the record of the death of the old bishop Polycarpus is the earliest description of a martyrdom	
	160–220 Tertullian describes the ritual of baptism	
	185–254 Origen states that infant baptism dates back to the time of the apostles	
	c.200 The gospels of Peter, Thomas, Mary, and others are now considered apocryphal	**c.200** Beginning of the recording of the *Puranas*, an Indian work of encyclopedic proportions
217–222 Pope Callixtus II	**217–222** Callixtus believes that all sins must be forgiven	**220** End of the Han dynasty in China
	c.225 The Christians constitute one of the largest religious communities in the Roman Empire	
235–285 Anarchy in the Roman Empire	**235–285** Christianity attracts a great number of followers, causing an expansion of the communities and a decrease in personal contact; construction of the catacombs in Rome	
248–251 Under the emperor Decius, all inhabitants of the empire must make offerings to the Roman gods; violent persecutions of the Christians	**c.250** Paul of Thebes flees from persecution into the desert	
257 Edict against the Church, confiscation of property; Church officials are summarily executed	**c.250–356** St. Anthony of Alexandria	
	251 Restoration of the Christian Church after the persecutions	
268 Gallienus discontinues the persecutions and restores the Church's possessions	**c.260–300** The problem of penitent apostates troubles the Church; there are many new converts, especially in the army	
284 Diocletian becomes emperor		
292 The Roman army is purged of Christians	**c.290–347** Pachomius draws up a set of rules for Christians to live by	**316–589** The sciences flourish in China
303 Persecutions of Christians, especially in administrative positions; deputy emperor of the West does not pursue the persecutions seriously	**c.300–350** A massive number of pious Christians withdraw from society	
305 Diocletian abdicates, Galerius succeeds him		
311 Edict of tolerance, making it legal for the first time to be a Christian		

| Prehistory | Antiquity | Middle Ages | Renaissance | Modern History | Contemporary History |

CHRISTIANITY POLITICAL HISTORY	CHRISTIANITY CULTURAL HISTORY	EVENTS IN THE REST OF THE WORLD
312 Constantine the Great conquers Rome **313** Edict of Milan; Christians are entitled to practice their religion freely **324** Constantine becomes sole ruler of the Roman Empire **325** Constantine calls the first Council of Nicaea	**312** The emperor Constantine testifies to his belief in Christianity; preferential treatment of the Church; converts swell the Christian ranks **324** Constantine donates vast possessions to the Church and, in particular, to the city of Rome **325** Disagreement concerning the mystery of the Trinity; according to the Council of Nicaea, the Son is equal to the Father; pagan customs are outlawed **329–379** Basil of Caesarea, who formulates a monastic rule **331** Divorce among Christians is permitted only under exceptional circumstances	**320–499** All of northern India is ruled by the Gupta dynasty
337 Death of Constantine 	**337** Constantine is baptized on his deathbed **337–361** The emperor Constans publicly speaks against paganism, but rules that outside the cities temples to the gods must be respected **337–400** Christianity has expanded too much to retain a personal approach; enormous churches are built; the emperors favor an increase of the hierarchy within the Church; the episcopal hierarchy is headed by the patriarchs of Rome, Antioch, and Alexandria **340–397** Ambrose, bishop of Milan, writes *De officiis ministrorum* **c.340** St. Anthony visits St. Paul in the desert **342–420** Jerome, a church father, translates the Old Testament into Latin **347** Nine monastic communities are living according to the rule of Pachomius **c.350** The teachings of Christianity are condensed into a theology that includes the adoration of the crucified messiah; a vast system of martyrs, bishops, and priests is established **354–430** St. Augustine of Hippo, a church father	**335–375** Flowering of India under Chandragupta II **c.350** Chinese influence on Japan and Korea
361–363 Julian the Apostate reigns as emperor **364–375** The emperor Valentinian I returns to the policies of Constantine **366–384** Pope Damasus I **379** Theodosius I becomes emperor **392** The Frankish general Arbogast rebels against Theodosius **394** Theodosius defeats Arbogast **395** Theodosius definitively divides his empire into two parts	**360–435** John Cassian, the lawgiver of monasticism, founds the monastery of St. Victor at Marseilles **c.360** St. Martin becomes bishop of Tours **361–363** The emperor Julian tries to restore paganism **374** Infanticide is made illegal **379** The emperor Theodosius unambiguously endorses the edicts of the Council of Nicaea **379–395** During Theodosius's reign, the altars and sanctuaries of pagan gods are destroyed **381** The bishop of the new capital of Constantinople is given the title of patriarch; all animal sacrifices to the gods are banned **386** Augustine is converted to Christianity **390** Augustine writes his *Confessions* **392** All pagan cults are officially outlawed	
c.400 The pope is the most important man in Rome **410** Sack of Rome by Alaric **440–461** Pope Leo I the Great prevents Rome from being conquered by Attila **451** Fourth Council of Chalcedon **476** The last western Roman emperor is dethroned by the Teutons **493** Italy in hands of the Ostrogoths	**413** Augustine writes *De Civitate Dei (The City of God)* **418** Condemnation of Pelagius by Church **c.450** St. Patrick preaches Christianity in Ireland **451** At the Council of Chalcedon, the pope and the patriarch are placed on the same hierarchical level **480–547** Benedict of Norcia **529** Plato's Academy is closed	**c.400** Beginning of the Yamato Empire in Japan **441** Attila becomes the sole ruler of the Huns **c.470** Ephtalites in northern India **c.500** Battles rage among the Mayan city-states **511** Death of Clovis, king of the Franks
527–565 Justinian is emperor of the Eastern Roman Empire **553** Conquest of Italy by Justinian **556–561** Pope Pelagius II **568** Italy conquered by the Lombards; Rome is governed by a city prefecture and the pope **590–604** Pope Gregory I the Great; the papacy regains international prestige	**c.540** Benedict establishes a monastic rule at Monte Cassino **c.550** Irish monasteries are centers of Christian culture **590–604** *Moralia in Job (Morals in the Book of Job)* by Gregory the Great **597** The king of England is baptized by St. Augustine of Canterbury **634** Irish monks found a monastery at Lindisfarne in England **664** The Synod of Whitby opts for the Roman computation of Easter **731** Bede's *Historia Ecclesiastica Gentis Anglorum (Ecclesiastical History of the English Nation)*	**552** Monks introduce Buddhism to Japan **589** The Great Wall of China is repaired **606–647** Harsha Empire, India **618** Start of the Tang dynasty in China **632** Death of Muhammad **712** Beginning of Islamic influence in India **732** Charles Martel defeats the Muslim army at Poitiers

400 —
500 —
600 —

| Prehistory | Antiquity | Middle Ages | Renaissance | Modern History | Contemporary History |

Glossary

ahimsa (Sanskrit: nonviolence) Buddhist doctrine of nonviolence and adopted by Gandhi.

Ambrose, Saint (c.340–397) bishop of Milan; doctor of the Church; opposed Arianism; brought Roman emperor Theodosius I to repentance for the massacre of Thessalonians.

Amidism Buddhist religious sect, also called Pure Land, originating in China.

anatman (Sanskrit: no soul) Buddhist concept that individual soul does not exist.

angels spirits venerated by Christians.

Anglo-Saxon Church integration of Irish and Christian practices and rites in Britannia.

Anthony, Saint (c.251–c.350) early Egyptian Christian hermit and first Christian monk; subject of the first hagiography (saint's life).

Antiochus I Soter (the Preserver) king of Syria (c.280–262 BC) son of Seleucus I, general, successor of Alexander the Great.

Antiochus III, the Great king of Syria (223–187 BC); son of Seleucus II; brother of and successor to Seleucus III; the most important Seleucid; defeated Ptolemy V; seized Palestine and Lebanon; defeated by the Romans at Thermopylae and at Magnesia (Turkey).

Antiochus IV Epiphanes (the Illustrious) king of Syria (175–164 BC); son of Antiochus III; defeated Egyptian kings Ptolemy VI and Ptolemy VII; seized Jerusalem, prohibited Judaism in favor of the worship of Greek gods; ousted by the Maccabees at the end of the Jewish Revolt.

Adeodatus (Latin: gift from God) natural son of Augustine

apologias defenses by Christian scholars against pagan and Jewish philosophers.

apostles disciples of Jesus Christ, founders of the first Christian community after his death.

arhats Hindu or Buddhist holy men.

Arianism Christian doctrine named for its author, Arius, that denied the divine nature of Jesus Christ; condemned at the Council of Nicaea.

Arius (c.256–336) native of Libya, Alexandrian priest who articulated the Arian doctrine named for him.

Artaxerxes I king of Persia (465–425 BC).

Asoka (270–232 BC) king in northern India who contributed to the spread of Buddhism across India and beyond.

ashram refuge.

Athanasius, Saint (c.293–373) Christian bishop, theologian, and doctor of the Church; noted for his fourth-century opposition to the Arian heresy.

Augustine of Hippo, Saint (354–430) Christian convert, bishop, and preeminent theologian, doctor of the Church; author of the apologia *De Civitate Dei* (*The City of God*), the autobiography *Confessiones* (*Confessions*), *Epistles*, and treatises.

Augustine of Canterbury, Saint archbishop of Canterbury (598–604); converted Anglo-Saxons in Britannia; founded Roman Catholic Christianity in Kent, competing with Irish Christianity; established Canterbury as the administrative center of the Anglo-Saxon Church.

Babylonian exile period from c.587–536 BC in which the elite of Judah, after being conquered by the Babylonian king Nebuchadnezzar, lived in Babylon.

baptism (Latin: dipping in) Christian ceremony admitting individuals into Christianity by immersion or sprinkling with water to symbolically wash away original sin.

Basil, Saint (c.329–379) Greek bishop of Caesarea; Cappadocian church father and eastern doctor of the Church; established monasticism in the east, emphasizing asceticism and obedience, spiritual growth, and the study of theological works.

Bede the Venerable, Saint (c.673–735) English Benedictine monk and scholar, author of *Historia Ecclesiastica Gentis Anglorum* (*Ecclesiastical History of the English People*), detailing English history from Roman occupation to 731.

Benedictine monastic order founded by Benedict; stresses communal living, obedience to an abbot, physical labor, study of the sciences, communal property and meals, and the avoidance of unnecessary speech.

Benedict of Nursia, Saint (c.480–547) monk from Umbria (Italy); founder of the Benedictine monastic order and the monastery of Monte Cassino; the father of western monasticism.

Bhagavad-Gita Hindu poem composed around 200 BC and added to the Mahabharata, wherein the importance of action versus reflection is discussed during a meeting between Krishna and Arjuna.

bishops seen by Christians as successors to the apostles; held the highest authority in the *ecclesia* (church), deriving their power from the support of emperors. The bishop of Rome is the pope.

bodhisattva (Sanskrit: enlightened being) a potential Buddha, one who chooses to delay entering the state of nirvana in order to help all sentient beings; under the Mahayana doctrine, a bliss-bearing supernatural entity.

Brahma paramount Indian god, preacher of the *Vedas*, appears in Hinduism as part of a trinity of Brahman the Creator, Vishnu the Restorer, and Shiva the Destroyer.

Brahman divine absolute reality in Hinduism and the earlier Brahmanism.

Brahmanism ancient Indian religion; detailed in the scriptures called *Brahmanas* and *Vedas* of the sixth century BC.

brahmin (Sanskrit: priest) highest Hindu caste.

Buddha (the Enlightened One) the title of Siddhartha Gautama, founder of Buddhism; also anyone attaining enlightenment.

Buddhism religion founded by Siddhartha Gautama, called the Buddha; rejected much of Hinduism, including priestly authority, the Vedic scriptures, sacrificial practices, and the caste system. Its goal is *nirvana*, release from all desire and from the cycle of life, death, and rebirth; major schools are Theravada and Mahayana.

Buddhist era fourth to ninth centuries AD, when Buddhism spread from India to central, eastern, and southeast Asia.

Caesarea city in southern Syria expanded by Herod the Great into a fashionable metropolis with temples, amphitheaters, and a major trade center.

Caesaropapism the special relationship between church and state.

Cassian, John also called Johannes Eremita or Johannes Massiliensis (360–435); spent fifteen years as a hermit in Egypt; brought eastern monasticism west; theological opponent of Augustine; wrote on monasticism.

caste system division of Indian society into four hereditary social groups based on occupation: brahmins (priests), kshatriyas (warriors and kings), vaishyas (landowners), and shudras (servants).

catacombs underground corridors outside Rome where Christians buried their dead and assembled in secret during persecution.

cenobites hermits who sought personal solitude within a common monastic life, called *koinos bios* in Greek.

Children of God term used by Mahatma Gandhi for the untouchables, lowest-ranking people of Hindu society.

Christ (Greek: Messiah) name accorded Jesus of Nazareth.

Christianity monotheistic religion founded by followers of Jesus Christ, who consider him the son of God, sent to earth to take on the sins of humankind through his death and resurrection. During Theodosius's reign

997

Christianity became the state religion.

Christians followers of Jesus Christ; early Christians gathered for communal meals and to commemorate Jesus' death.

Chuang-tzu (c.369–286 BC) philosopher, teacher; important proponent of Daoism.

Confucianism Chinese philosophy founded by Kong-fu-tse; focused on human ethics within an ordered society; state ideology of the Han dynasty; spread to rest of Asia.

Constantine the Great (c. AD 274–337) Roman emperor (306–337); sole ruler of the empire in 324; reorganized imperial administration; with the Edict of Milan, he legitimized Christianity, converting to it on his deathbed.

Constantius II Roman emperor (351–361), second son of Constantine the Great.

Council of Chalcedon (451) convocation of church leaders near Constantinople leading to the first schism of the Christian Church over the relative status of the pope in Rome and the patriarch of Constantinople.

Council of Nicaea (325) convocation of bishops of the Roman Empire, a forum to discuss church matters, including the nature of Jesus Christ. It rejected Arianism.

Daode Jing (*Tao-te-Ching, The Classic of the Way of Power*), the earliest Daoist scripture, attributed to Laozi (Lao-tzu, c.500 BC), although written about 200–100 BC; probably his students' record of his teachings.

Daoism (Taoism) Chinese philosophy originated by Laozi (Lao-tzu) about 500 BC; emphasizes inner harmony with nature and yielding to the Dao (Tao, the Way), the natural flow of things.

darshanas classical schools of Hinduism.

deacons assistants to the apostles and bishops, usually prominent citizens who devoted their time to the followers of Christianity.

Dead Sea Scrolls rolls of parchment found in AD 1947 near the Dead Sea; contain the earliest biblical texts known, with Essene moral codes and theological comments; probably hidden by Essenes during Jewish revolt.

Decius Roman emperor (249–251) notable for his attempts at reform and the first systematic persecution of Christians.

De Temporum Ratione (*On the Reckoning of Time*, 725) written by Bede the Venerable; introduced the concept of dating events AD (*Anno domini*, the year of the Lord) and BC (before Christ).

dhamma (Sanskrit: the way to enlightenment) the teachings of Buddha.

dharma (Sanskrit: right social behavior) Hindu concept of correct behavior in line with the cosmic order.

dukka (Sanskrit: suffering) the underlying condition of existence, in Buddhism.

ecclesiae Christian communities, governed by a bishop, where theological and liturgical issues were discussed; eventually met in special meeting halls (churches). *Ecclesiae* of the third century presented themselves as funeral societies to gain legal status.

Edict of Milan (AD 313) proclaimed by Emperor Constantine in the west and Galerius in the east, it legalized Christian worship.

Eightfold Path Buddhist concept of the way to spiritual improvement: right views, right intention, right speech, right action, right livelihood, right effort, right mindfulness, and right concentration.

eremites hermits or recluses who lived solitary lives of asceticism. Many early Christians withdrew to such a life in the desert to acquire personal sanctity, a move that led to monasticism.

Essenes Jewish religious brotherhoods that maintained a monastic way of life in communal settlements at the beginning of the first century BC. In all likelihood, Essenes wrote the *Dead Sea Scrolls*.

evangelists nominal authors of the gospels: Matthew, Mark, Luke, and John.

Four Noble Truths Buddhist concept that existence is suffering, and suffering is caused by ignorance of the true nature of reality, leading to attachment and craving for worldly pleasures; following the Eightfold Path can end suffering.

Galerius Roman emperor (305–311); continued the Christian persecution Diocletian had begun, closing the catacombs and sacking churches. In 311 he issued an edict of tolerance, effectively legalizing Christianity.

Gautama, Siddhartha (c.480–400 BC) a prince of the Shakya clan; called the Buddha, founder of Buddhism.

Gospels the first four books of the New Testament, named after and attributed to Matthew, Mark, Luke, and John; compiled after the crucifixion of Jesus Christ from the work of many people.

Gratian (359–383) full name Flavius Gratianus, western Roman emperor (367–383); coemperor with his father Valentinian I until the latter's death in 375, then with his half brother Valentinian II.

Gregorian chants ritual plain songs instituted by Pope Gregory I; used in the Roman Catholic Church; unharmonized, unaccompanied, and sung without meter.

Gregory I, the Great, Saint (c.540–604) pope (590–604); last of the four original doctors of the Church; defended Rome against the Lombards; had England Christianized, giving new momentum to Christianity in Europe.

hagiography biography of a saint; featured a moral message and visions, prophecies, and miracles testifying to the saint's piety.

Han dynasty (Chinese) (206 BC–AD 220) period where Confucianism became state religion.

heaven Christian place where saved souls live eternally in the presence of God.

Helena, Saint (c.248–328) wife of the Roman emperor Constantius I and mother of Constantine the Great, emperor of Rome.

hell place where souls of the damned live eternally, according to Christian belief; portrayed as eternal fire, ruled by the devil.

Herod the Great king of Palestine (37–4 BC) under the Romans.

Hilary of Poitiers, Saint (c.315–367) pagan convert to Christianity, doctor of the Church, bishop of Poitiers; noted for his lifelong opposition to the Arian heresy.

Hinayana (the Lesser Vehicle) disparaging term for Theravada Buddhism.

Hinduism predominant religion in India, originating from Brahmanism; characterized by belief in many gods headed by Brahma, Shiva, and Vishnu.

Irish Christianity founded by Patrick around AD 400, centered around monasteries that were also Celtic cultural centers.

Jerome, Saint (c.345–c.420) father and doctor of Church; translated Bible into Latin version called the Vulgate; converted many aristocrats, including women; founded a monastery and a nunnery in Bethlehem.

Jesus Christ (c.6 BC–AD 30) Jewish religious leader crucified as a rebel; his followers were the first Christians.

Jewish Revolt uprising against the Roman procurator by radical Jewish factions, primarily zealots, from AD 66–70. Through a war of annihilation, the Roman armies restored order, captured Jerusalem in 70 and destroyed the Temple.

John the Baptist Jewish preacher who preached and baptized on the banks of the Jordan River; proclaimed the coming of the Messiah; executed by Herod Antipas.

Julian the Apostate (Flavius Claudius Julianus) (c.331–363) Roman emperor (361–363); denounced Christianity; attempted to restore worship of the traditional Roman gods after the adoption of Christianity by Constantine the Great.

karma (Sanskrit: fate, work) one's acts and their consequences in a subsequent existence. In Buddhism, karma is considered the result of actions which define kind of rebirth that occurs, not as punishment, but for evolution; in Hinduism, karma means cause and effect, bearing in this life the consequences of actions taken in previous lives.

Kong-fu-tse (Confucius) (551–479 BC) Chinese philosopher and founder of Confucianism.

kshatriyas (kings and warriors) second-ranking Hindu caste.

Laozi (Lao-tze) (c.500 BC) Chinese philosopher, founder of Daoism. His philosophy is recorded in the Daoist scriptures called the *Daode Jing (Tao-te-ching, The Classic of the Way of Power)*.

legalism pragmatic Chinese philosophy, strongest over the third century BC; absolute state rules supersede the individual.

liturgy prescribed form of Christian worship.

Lombards Teutonic tribes from Central Europe who conquered Italy in AD 568.

Maccabees Jewish movement fighting for political autonomy, founded to obtain freedom of religion; freed Palestine from Seleucid rule; established a monarchy of high priests in Jerusalem.

Mahabharata epic poem of Hinduism, composed between 400 BC and AD 200; describes cousins vying for control in the kingdom of the Kurus. The *Bhagavad-Gita* is included in the *Mahabharata*.

Mahayana (Sanskrit: great vehicle) the largest school of Buddhism; reveres the bodhisattva who has achieved enlightenment and Buddhahood and is reborn to help others find the Way (salvation); considers Buddha the incarnation of absolute truth.

Manichaeism Persian philosophy named for its third-century founder, Mani. He saw himself as final prophet in line that included Zoroaster, Buddha, and Jesus. It postulated a world of perpetual conflict between good and evil, the transmigration of souls, and a celibate, vegetarian "elect" who could attain the Kingdom of Light after death. Lower "auditors" who served them could only attain possible rebirth as an elect.

Martin of Tours, Saint (316–397) bishop of Tours; one of the founders of monasticism in the west; patron saint of France for his conversion efforts in Gaul.

martyrs Christians who persisted in their faith despite persecution, torture, and death; believed to attain salvation upon death, they were often venerated.

meditation deep and continuous concentration, used by a number of mystical traditions to bypass the mind and focus reflection on (divine) truth.

Mengzi (Mencius) (327–289 BC) disciple of Confucius who considered peace and prosperity the result of kings acting in an ethical manner. Believing people inherently good, he insisted that government be exercised on their behalf. When it was not, subjects had the right to depose it.

Messiah in Judaism, the savior sent by Yahweh (God); in Christianity, it is Jesus.

Mimamsa (inquiry) orthodox school of Hinduism that explained the *Vedas* and continued the Brahmanical offerings.

monastery ascetic community of monks led by an abbot under permanent, strict regulations. In the east, Basil was the founder of monasticism, in the west, Benedict of Nursia.

Nehemiah Jewish governor who returned from exile in Babylon in 444 BC and, with Ezra, arranged for Jewish self-rule. He instituted a civil government, while Ezra introduced religious reforms. They drew up a set of Jewish laws, including the kosher rules on hygiene, diet, and the Sabbath.

Nero (Nero Claudius Caesar Drusus Germanicus, originally named Lucius Domitius Ahenobarbus) (AD 37–68) Roman emperor (AD 54–69); noted for initiating the first major persecutions of Christians, the great fire of Rome that he was rumored to have set himself in 64, and a reign of malevolent disorder. Proclaimed a public enemy by the Roman Senate, he committed suicide on June 9, AD 68.

Nestorius (died c. AD 451) Syrian monk who disputed the Greek title *Theotokos (Mother of God)* for Mary, insisting she was the mother of Jesus, not of God.

Nestorianism teaching of fourth–century Nestorius condemned as heresy by the Council of Ephesus (431).

New Testament the part of the Bible containing the teachings of Jesus Christ and his disciples, including the four Gospels, the Epistles of Paul, the Acts of the Apostles, and the Revelation of St. John.

nirvana (Sanskrit: "blow out") the state of perfect inner peace and enlightenment, when desire is extinguished and the cycle of birth, death, and rebirth ends. In Hinduism, the word refers to blowing out the flame of life. To Buddha, it meant blowing out the fires of desire, hatred, and ignorance, reaching a condition of complete detachment.

Nyaya (analysis) Hindu philosophy of salvation achieved by true knowledge, logic, observation, and comparison.

Origen (c.185–254) Alexandrian Christian theologian.

Pachomius (c.290–346) Christian hermit; founded monastic commune in Egypt.

patriarch male head of family or clan; a prominent bishop of the early Christian Church; eventually used as title of the head of the Eastern Orthodox Church.

patrimonium Petri (Peter's estate) tracts of land in Italy acquired by the popes to pay for papal living expenses.

Paul, Saint (c. AD 3–62) Saul of Tarsus, Jewish scribe, later disciple of Jesus Christ;

first Christian theologian, his letters are part of the New Testament.

Pelagius (AD 400) Roman-British monk who denied the doctrine of original sin and the need for infant baptism; preached Christian asceticism and morality.

Pelagianism Christian doctrine of Pelagius; considered human corruption not inborn, denying original sin and the need for infant baptism; humans could attain salvation by their own efforts; well accepted in southern Italy and Sicily but declared heretical by Augustine and the Church.

peregrination (wandering) practice by Irish monks of wandering the countryside and spreading Christianity, adopted by the Anglo-Saxon Church (notably the monks Willibrord and Boniface).

Pharisees orthodox Jews, organized in the second century BC as the Hasidim; rigidly observed the written law but also accepted the validity of the oral law that had developed as scholars strove to interpret tradition.

Philo Hebreus (c.25 BC–AD 45) Jewish scholar from Alexandria; contended Greek philosophers derived ideas from Jewish sources.

Polycarpus of Smyrna earliest recorded Christian martyr, burned to death c.AD 156.

pope bishop and patriarch of Rome, head of the Roman Catholic Church.

praefectus urbi (Latin: prefect of the city) the official assigned by the Byzantine emperor to head the administration of Rome.

Prajnaparamita Sutra Mahayana Buddhist addition to the *Theravada* text, the *Tripitaka*.

pratityasamutpada (Sanskrit: dependent origin) Hindu doctrine; each link in chain of existence is determined by previous one and becomes prerequisite for next.

predestination concept that everything that happens is foreordained by God, including the soul's salvation or damnation.

Ptolemy I king of Egypt (323–285 BC); founder of the Ptolemaic dynasty.

Ptolemy II Ptolemy Philadelphus (brotherly); king of Egypt (285-246 BC); son of Ptolemy I.

Ptolemy V Epiphanes (Illustrious) (c.210–181 BC) king of Egypt (205 181 BC).

Puranas (ancient stories) extensive Hindu texts composed between the first centuries AD and the Middle Ages.

rabbi (Hebrew: my master) ordained teacher of Jewish law; authorized to perform marriages and decide questions of ritual and law.

Ramayana short Hindu epic concerning the adventures of Rama, king of Ayodha, also considered an avatar of Vishnut, and a Hindu deity.

Roman Catholic Church term now used for the Christian church governed by bishops and the pope in Rome; became the center of western Christianity in the Middle Ages.

Sadducees from the name Zadok, Old Testament priest under Kings David and Solomon (2 Samuel 15:24–29); aristocratic school of religious thought and political party in the first century BC in the Jewish state; accepted only the written Torah as binding law; did not believe in personal immortality or the existence of spirits.

saint individual recognized by the Christian Church as having lived or died in an exemplary manner, distinguished by piety; venerated by some Christians and considered able to intercede for faithful and effect miracles; each saint has fixed day of commemoration.

Samaritans inhabitants of Samaria in central Palestine; came into conflict with the Jews returning from the Babylonian captivity starting in 536 BC.

Sankhya (count) school of Hindu philosophy based on dualism, the theory that reality is divided into matter (*prakrit*) and the soul or spirit (*purusha*).

samsara (Sanskrit) cycle of birth, death, and rebirth, taken from the *Upanishads*.

sangha (Sanskrit) community of Buddhist mendicant monks, founded by Buddha's first disciples, who achieve own nirvana through ascet cism and teach the *dharma*.

Sanhedrin the Jewish state council of 71 priests and religious leaders responsible for all religious and civil functions; presided over by the high priest; abolished with the destruction of Jerusalem in AD 70.

Septuagint (Latin: 70) the 72 scholars who produced the Greek translation of Jewish religious writings; commissioned by Ptolemy Philadelphus; customarily abbreviated LXX, the roman numerals for seventy.

Shakti (power) Hindu female creative and destroying energy of God; embodied as mother goddess and bride of Shiva; pre-Arian religion of the Mother Goddess had a resurgence during the fifth century AD when the feminine creative principle was worshiped with a great variety of rituals.

Shankara (c.788–820) Indian philosopher who believed in monism or nondualism, called *Advaita Vedanta*. He insisted on the identity of atman (soul) and Brahman.

Shiva Hindu god of destruction and reproduction; member of the Hindu trinity with Vishnu and Brahma; his worshipers are known as *shaivas*. He frequently manifests in his female aspects: Parvati and Kali.

simony the buying and selling of Christian ecclesiastical offices for money.

soteriology Christian doctrine of saving through healing.

shudras Hindu caste of servants.

svadharma (Sanskrit: personal dharma) Hindu concept that holds the individual is born to a certain social level and occupation and should work within it to the best of his ability in order to fulfill his dharma.

Tantrism religious sects in Hinduism and Buddhism based on tantras; followers sought unity of matter and soul, male and female principles, through magic, ritual, and yoga.

tantras (Sanskrit: warp, as in weaving) esoteric Indian texts used in both Buddhist and Hindu Tantric sects; concern symbolism, ritual, and magic, presented as dialogue between Shiva and his consort Parvati.

Tao-te-Ching See *Daode Jing*.

Taoism *See* Daoism.

Tertullian (c.160–230) Quintus Septimius Florens Tertullianus; Latin church father.

Theodosius I (c.346–395) full name Flavius Theodosius, called Theodosius the Great; Roman emperor of the east (379–395) and of the west (394–395), last ruler of a united Roman Empire; prohibited all religions except Christianity.

Theravada (the Way of the Elders) Buddhist school of *Sravakayana* (vehicle of the disciples); disparagingly called *Hinayana* (little vehicle) by advocates of Mahayana Buddhism; emphasizes self-reliant striving against desire; emphasizes monasticism.

Tibet country north of India; developed its own form of Buddhism (Lamaism) in the eighth century AD.

transmigration Hindu concept of the atman moving through the cycle of phenomenal existence.

Tree of Enlightenment the bo tree under which Siddhartha Gautama attained enlightenment.

Tripitaka (Sanskrit: three baskets) the scriptures of Theravada Buddhism; refers to the baskets used by first-century BC Sri Lankan Buddhist monks to hold palm-leaf scrolls.

Vaishesika (the school of individual characteristics) school of Hindu philosophy that complements the *Nyaya*; classifies the forms of reality.

Valerian Publius Licinius Valerianus (died in Persian captivity AD 260) emperor of Rome (253–260).

Vaipulya Sutras Mahayana Buddhist addition to the *Tripitaka*.

vaishyas Hindu caste of tradespeople and farmers.

Vedanta (end of the *Vedas*) school of Hindu

philosophy; focused on union with Brahman and salvation of the material world.

Vedas earliest sacred Hindu scriptures; four collections of sacrificial hymns taken over from oral tradition of Brahmanism and prescriptions for ritual: the Rig-Veda, the *Samaveda*, the *Yajurveda*, and the *Atharvaveda*. Vedic literature also includes the *Brahmanas* that define the rituals and mythology, the *Aran-yakas (Forest Treatises)*, and the *Upanishads* (later theological and more mystical interpretation of the earlier works).

Vishnu Hindu god called the Preserver; forms a trinity with Brahma and Shiva; takes human form as Krishna.

Vulgate (Latin: popular or common) fourth-century Latin translation and organization of the Bible by Jerome; the authorized version in the Roman Catholic Church.

Warring States period (480–221 BC) Chinese era when Zhou dynasty disintegrated into vying politically independent principalities.

yoga (Sanskrit: yoke) Hindu school of philosophy and practice involving physical and mental discipline to restore the balance of spiritual energy; intense concentration attained by prescribed postures and exercises, including controlled breathing, to gain mystical union with Brahman.

zealots first-century AD orthodox Jewish sect that resisted Roman domination in Palestine and demanded social reforms; some took guerilla action.

Zen Buddhism Buddhist school originally developed in China (Ch'in in Chinese), later in Japan; a blending of Mahayana Buddhism and Daoism.

Zhuangzi (Zhuang-tse) (369–268 BC) Chinese Daoist philosopher who reinterpreted the *Daode Jing (Tao-te-ching)* to make Daoism accessible to a wider audience.

Bibliography

The Buddha
Carrithers, M. *The Buddha.* Oxford, 1986.
Herbert, P. M. *The Life of the Buddha.* London, 1993.
Holy Places of the Buddha. Berkeley, 1994.
Kalupahana, D. J. *The Way of Siddharta.* Lanham, 1987.
Klimkeit, H. J. *Der Buddha.* Stuttgart, 1990.
Morup, S. *The Date of the Buddha's Mahaparinirvana.* New Delhi, 1991.
Seth, V. *Study of Biographies of the Buddha.* New Delhi, 1992.
Withshire, M. G. *Ascetic Figures before and in Early Buddhism.* Berlin/New York, 1990.

Buddhism
Frederic, L. *Buddhism.* Paris, 1995.
Gombrich, R. *Theravada Buddhism.* London, 1988.
Reat, N. Ross. *Buddhism: A History.* Berkeley, 1994.
Swearer, D. *The Buddhist World of SE Asia.* New York, 1995.
Thurman, R. A. F. *Essential Tibetan Buddhism.* San Francisco, 1995.
Zwalf, W., ed. *Buddhism: Art and Faith.* London, 1985.

Hinduism
Basham, A. L. *The Origins and Development of Classical Hinduism.* Boston, 1989.
Cross, S. *The Elements of Hinduism.* Shaftesbury, 1994.
Dange, S. A. *Rigveda Hymns and Ancient Thought.* New Delhi, 1992.
Daweewarn, D. *Brahmanism in SE Asia.* New Delhi, 1987.
Gonda, J. *A History of Indian Literature.* Wiesbaden, 1975.
—. *Visnuism and Sivaism.* London, 1970.
Kanitkar, V. P., and Cole, W. O. *Hinduism.* London, 1995.
Klostermaier, K. K. *A Survey of Hinduism.* New York, 1994.
Van Nooten and Holland. *Rig Veda.* Cambridge, 1994.
Shirvastava, V. S. *Hinduism in SE Asia.* New Delhi, 1989.

Early Chinese Thinkers
Girardot, N. J. *Myth and Meaning in Early Taoism.* Berkeley, 1980.
Kohn, L., ed. *The Taoist Experience.* Albany, NY, 1993.
Kohn, L. *Early Chinese Mysticism.* Princeton, 1992.
Nikkilae, P. *Early Confucianism.* Helsinki, 1992.
Rozman, G., ed. *The East Asian Region.* Princeton, 1990.
Schipper, K. *The Taoist Body.* Berkeley, 1993.
Seidl, A. *Taoismus.* Tokyo, 1990.

The Jewish People
Avi-Yonah, M. *The Jews under Roman and Byzantine Rule.* Jerusalem, 1984.
Bickerman, B. *The God of the Maccabees.* Leiden, 1979.
Cantor, N. *The Sacred Chain.* London, 1995.
McCullough, W. S. *The History and Literature of the Palestinian Jews.* Toronto, 1975.
Grant, M. *Herod the Great.* London, 1971.
Harrington, D. *The Maccabean Revolt.* Wilmington, 1988.
Modrzejewski, J. Meleze. *The Jews of Egypt.* Edinburgh, 1995.
Schurer, E. *The History of the Jewish People in the Age of Jesus Christ.* Edinburgh, 1973.
Smallwood, E. M. *The Jews under Roman Rule from Pompey to Diocletian.* Leiden, 1981.

The Beginning of Christianity
Bornkamm, G. *Paul.* New York, 1971.
Gager, J. G. *Kingdom and Community.* Englewood Cliffs, 1975.
Hering, J. *The First Epistle of St. Paul.* London, 1962.
Van der Loos, H. *The Miracles of Jesus.* Leiden, 1968.
Meeks, W. A. *The First Urban Christians.* London, 1983.
Sanders, E. P. *Jesus and Judaism.* Philadelphia, 1985.
Zeitlin, I. M. *Jesus and the Judaism of His Time.* Cambridge, 1989.

Christianity Comes of Age
Barnes, T. D. *Early Christianity and the Roman Empire.* London, 1984.
Droge, A. J., and Tabor, J. D. *A Noble Death.* San Francisco, 1992.
Frend, W. *Martyrdom and Persecution in the Early Church.* New York, 1967.
—. *The Rise of Christianity.* London, 1984.
Grant, R. *Augustus to Constantine.* San Francisco, 1990.
Fox, R. Lane. *Pagans and Christians in the Mediterranean World.* London, 1986.
Markus, R. A. *Christianity in the Roman World.* London, 1974.
MacMullen, R. *Christianizing the Roman Empire.* New Haven, 1984.

The Fall of Paganism
Barnes, T. *Athansius and Constantine.* Cambridge, 1993.
Chadwick, H. *The Early Church.* Harmondsworth, 1967.
Frend, W. *The Rise of Christianity.* London, 1984.
Hillgarth, J. *Christianity and Paganism.* Philadelphia, 1986.
Laistner, M. L. W. *Christianity and Pagan Culture in the Late Roman Empire.* New York, 1951.
MacMullen, R. *Christianizing the Roman Empire.* New Haven, 1984.
—. *Constantine.* London, 1967.

Christian Theology and Popular Belief
Brown, P. *Augustine of Hippo: A Biography.* London, 1967.
Chadwick, H. B. *Augustine: Past Masters.* Oxford, 1986.
Evans, G. R. *Augustine on Evil.* Cambridge, 1982.
Gregory, P. T. E. *Vox Populi.* Columbus, 1977.

Markus, R. A. *The End of Ancient Christianity*. Cambridge, 1990.
—. *Saeculum*. Cambridge, 1988.
—. *Augustine*. New York, 1972.
Marrou, H. I. *Décadence Romain*. Paris, 1977.

Monasticism
Bims, J. *Ascetics and Ambassadors of Christ*. New York, 1994.
Brown, P. *The Cult of the Saints*. Chicago, 1981.
—. *The Body and Society*. New York, 1988.
Cameron, A., and Kuhrt, A. *Images of Women in Late Antiquity*. Detroit, 1983.
Chitty, D. W. *The Desert a City*. Oxford, 1966.
Meinardus, O. F. A. *Monks and Monasteries of the Egyptian Deserts*. Cairo, 1989.
Prinz, F. *Askese und Kultur*. Munchen, 1980.
Rousseau, P. *Ascetics, Authority and the Church in the Age of Jerome and Cassian*. Oxford, 1978.
—. *Pachomonius*. Berkeley, 1985.

The Church in the West
Barley, M. *Christianity in Britain*. Leicester, 1968.
Chaney, W. A. *The Cult of Kingship in Anglo-Saxon England*. Berkeley, 1970.
Corse, T. *St. Patrick and Irish Christianity*. Minneapolis, 1979.
Harting, H. Mayr. *The Coming of Christianity to Anglo-Saxon England*. London, 1972.
Herrin, J. *The Formation of Christendom*. Princeton, 1987.
Houwen, L. *Beda venerabilis*. Groningen, 1996.
Myrtum, H. *The Origins of Early Irish Christianity*. London, 1992.
Straw, C. *Gregory the Great*. Berkeley, 1988.
Talbot, C. H. *The Anglo-Saxon Missionaries in Germany*. London, 1981.

Further Reading

Bazaz, Madhu. *Hinduism*. New York, 1991.

Booty, John E. *The Church in History*. San Francisco, 1984.

Brown, Stephen F. *Taoism*. New York, 1992.

Bull, Norman. *Founder of the Jews*. Chester Springs, PA, 1985.

Chatterjee, Dekjani. *The Elephant-headed God and Other Hindu Tales*. New York, 1995.

Cloony, Francis X. *Confucianism*. New York, 1992.

Dimont, Max L. *The Amazing Adventures of the Jewish People*. West Orange, NJ, 1984.

Hewitt, Catherine. *Buddhism*. New York, 1995.

Junior Encyclopedia of Judaica. New York, 1994.

Landaw, Jonathan. *The Story of Buddha*. Pomona, CA, 1979.

Levitin, Sonia. *Escape from Egypt*. New York, 1994.

Loverance, Rowena. *The Anglo-Saxons*. Jersey City, NJ, 1992.

Meyer, Carolyn. *Drummers of Jericho*. New York, 1995.

Reeve, John. *The Anglo-Saxons Activity Book*. New York, 1994.

Roth, Susan L. *Buddha*. New York, 1994.

Sacher, A. *History of the Jews*. New York, 1967.

Simms, George O. *St. Patrick*. Chester Springs, PA, 1994.

Srinivasan, A. V. *A Hindu Primer*. Glastonbury, CT, 1984.

Walker, Barbara G. *History of the Christian Church*. New York, 1984.

Yogeshananda, Swami. *Way of the Hindu*. New York, 1980.

Illustration Credits

Index

Text is indicated in roman type; illustrations are indicated in italic type.

Text is indicated in roman type; illustrations are indicated in italic type.

Text is indicated in roman type; illustrations are indicated in italic type.

the ancient capital of Ceylon   888
Majjhima   881
Mandalas   886
Mani (216–274?) Iranian founder of the Manichaean religion, a church advocating a dualistic doctrine that viewed the world as a fusion of spirit and matter   963–964, 997
Manichaeism   962–963, 997
Mantras   885–886
Manu, in Indian mythology the first man, and the legendary author of an important Sanskrit code of law, the Manu-smrti   894
Mara, evil god who tempted Buddha   873
Marcian   980
Marcus Tullius Cicero   962. *See* Cicero
Marius (157–86 BC) Roman general and politician   *950*
Mark (fl. first century AD) traditional author of the second Synoptic Gospel   926, 928, 930–931, 933, *933*, 956, 997
Marmoutier   975
Marseilles   975
Martin of Tours, Saint   (316–397) bishop of Tours; one of the founders of monasticism in the West   954, 975, *978*, 997
Martyrs   938, *942*, 955, 982, 997
Mary, mother of Jesus   926, *936*, 955–956, 997
Matsya, the "Noah" of the Hindus   894
Mattathias, Jewish priest, head of the Hasmonaean dynasty   918
Matthew, first in order of the four canonical Gospels and often called the "ecclesiastical" Gospel   926, 930–931, 933, *933*, 970, 997
Mauryan dynasty   886
Maxentius, Marcus Aurelius Valerius (d. 312), Roman emperor (reigned 306–312); his father, the emperor Maximian, abdicated with Diocletian (305)   943, *946*
Maximianus, Roman emperor (286–305)   *946*
Maya   *872*, 898
Meditation   873, 875, 878, 885–886, 894, 997
Mediterranean   934, 937
Mencius   902, 905–907, 997. *See* Mengzi
Menelaus, in Greek mythology, king of Sparta and the younger son of Atreus, king of Mycenae   918
Mengzi, (327–289) disciple of Confucius who considered peace and prosperity the result of kings acting in an ethical manner   905, 997
Mesopotamia   950
Messiah, in Judaism, the savior sent by Yahweh (God); in Christianity, it is Jesus   925, 928, 933–934, 997
Metropolis   941, 948, 962, 997
Michael, archangel   956, *965*, *972*
Middle Ages   *923*, 931, *967*, 997
Milan   942, 944, *948*, 949, 953–954, 962, *964*, 997
Milvian Bridge, place where Constantine defeated Maxentius (312)   944
Mimamsa   897, 997
Miniature   874, 894, 915, 926, 931, 934, 938–939, 955, 962, 966–969, 976, 979, 985
Moab   913
Modein   918
Mohenjo-Daro   889

Moksha   893
Monasteries   875, 877, 879, 881, 886, *928*, *967*, 969, 971–972, 975–976, 978, 984, 988, 990, 997
Mongolia   876
Monica, mother of St. Augustine   962
Monophysite   980
Monophysitism   980
Monotheism   913
Moses, Israelite lawgiver and leader   917, 964
Mudras   886
Muslims   985
Myanmar   888

Nala   891
Narasimha, appearance of Vishnu as the demon-defeating man-lion   894
Nataraja, four-handed dancing Hindu god   896
Nebuchadnezzar, king of Babylonia (588 BC)   914, 997
Nehemiah   Jewish governor who arranged for Jewish self-rule   916–917, 997
Nepal   876, *878*
Nero, Claudius Caesar Drusus Germanicus, originally named Lucius Domitius Ahenobarbus, Roman emperor (reigned 54–69)   923, 936, 955, 997
Nestorianism   997
Nestorius (d. c. 451) Syrian monk who disputed the Greek title Theotokos (Mother of God) for Mary   956, 997
Netherlands   990
New
- Testament   926, 933–934, 937, 946, 964, 974, 997
Nicaea   945–946, *953*, 954, 974, 997. *See* Council of Nicaea
Nicene Creed   945–946
Nicomedia   941, 945
Nile   968–969
Nirvana   871, *873*, 875–876, 879, 882, 884, 893–894, 997
Noah, hero of the biblical story of the flood in the Old Testament book of Genesis   894
Nobility   904, 926
Noble
- Eightfold Path   875
- Truth   874
North
- Sea   990
- Africa   960
Northumbria   990
Nyaya   900, 997

Old Testament   *913*, 919, *956*, 997
Omri, Israelite king (reigned 876–869 BC)   913
Origen (c.185–254) Alexandrian Christian theologian   956, 965, 997
Orthodox Church   997

Pachomius (c.290–346) Christian hermit; founded monastic commune in Egypt   969, *969*, 971–972, 997
Padmasambhava, Tibetan Slob-Dpon ("Teacher"), (fl. eighth century), legendary Indian Buddhist mystic who introduced

Tantric Buddhism to Tibet 886
Paganism   943–944, 948–949, 951, 953–954, 966
Palestine   915, 917–918, 920–921, 933–934, 965, 969, 972, 997
Pali   881
Pandava group of brothers led by the god Krishna   891
Papacy   980–981, 987
Parashu, sixth manifestation of Vishnu, a lumberjack who prevents the Kshatriyas from oppressing the Brahmans   894
Parvati, consort of Shiva   *894*, *896*, 897, 997
Pastoral care   984
Patanjali   900
Patna   875
Patriarch of Constantinople, bishop Eusebius of Nicomedia   945, 948, 997
Patricius, father of St. Augustine   962
Patrimonium Petri   997
Paul
Paul, Saint (c.3–62), Jewish scribe, later disciple of Jesus Christ; first Christian theologian, his letters are part of the New Testament   *933*, 933–934, 936–937, 955–956, 960–961, 967, 974, 997
Pelagianism   997
Pelagius (400) Roman-British monk who denied the doctrine of original sin and the need for infant baptism   964–966, 981, 997
Pelagius II, pope (reigned 579 to 590)   981
Pentateuch   915
Peregrination   997
Persecution of Christians   997
Persepolis   915
Persia   916–917, 925, 997
Persian Empire   914, 917
Persians   892, 950
Peter, original name Simeon, or Simon (d. c.64), disciple of Jesus Christ   927, 931, 933–934, 936, 938, 954–955, 974–975, 981, 997
Pharisees   919–920, 922, 926, 928, 930, 997
Philo Hebreus (c.25 BC–AD 45) Jewish scholar from Alexandria   997
Phoenicia   918
Phoenician   913
Pilate, Pontius, Roman prefect (governor or procurator) of Judaea (26–36) under emperor Tiberius; he presided at the trial of Jesus and gave the order for his crucifixion   929, 931, *931*
Pilgrimages   988
Pilgrims   *951*, *972*, 988
Plague   984, *986*
Plato, (c.429–347 BC) Athenian philosopher and disciple of Socrates   948
Platonism   954
Pliny, Latin in full Gaius Plinius Caecilius Secundus (b. 61 or 62), Roman author and administrator   936
Poetry   886, 891
Poitiers   975, 985, 997
Polycarpus of Smyrna, earliest recorded Christian martyr, burned to death (c. 156)   997
Pompey the Great, Latin in full Gnaeus Pompeius Magnus (b. 106–48 BC), one of the great statesmen and generals of the late Roman Republic   920

Text is indicated in roman type; illustrations are indicated in italic type.

Text is indicated in roman type; illustrations are indicated in italic type.

Text is indicated in roman type; illustrations are indicated in italic type.